Documents and Debates
Eighteenth-Century Europe

Documents and Debates
General Editor: John Wroughton, M.A., F.R.Hist.S.

Eighteenth-Century Europe

Leonard W. Cowie
M.A., Ph.D., F.R.Hist.S.

M
MACMILLAN

© Leonard W. Cowie 1989

All rights reserved. No reproduction, copy or transmission of this publication may be made without written permission.

No paragraph of this publication may be reproduced, copied or transmitted save with written permission or in accordance with the provisions of the Copyright Act 1956 (as amended), or under the terms of any licence permitting limited copying issued by the Copyright Licensing Agency, 33–4 Alfred Place, London WC1E 7DP

Any person who does any unauthorised act in relation to this publication may be liable to criminal prosecution and civil claims for damages.

First published 1989

Published by
MACMILLAN EDUCATION LTD
Houndmills, Basingstoke, Hampshire RG21 2XS
and London
Companies and representatives
throughout the world

Typeset by Wessex Typesetters
(Division of The Eastern Press Ltd)
Frome, Somerset

Printed in Hong Kong

British Library Cataloguing in Publication Data
Cowie, Leonard W. (Leonard Wallace), 1919–
Eighteenth century Europe.—(Documents and debates).
1. Europe, 1715–1815
I. Title II. Series
940.2'53
ISBN 0–333–46530–X

Contents

	General Editor's Preface	vii
	Acknowledgements	ix
	Europe in The Eighteenth Century	1
I	The Enlightenment	4
II	Church and State	16
III	The Scientific Revolution	29
IV	The Enlightened Despots	38
V	The Century's Wars	49
VI	The French Monarchy	64
VII	Habsburgs and Hohenzollerns	73
VIII	Russia and its Neighbours	83
IX	The French Revolution	95
X	Napoleon in France and Abroad	105

General Editor's Preface

This book forms part of a series entitled *Documents and Debates*, which is aimed primarily at sixth formers. The earlier volumes in the series each covered approximately one century of history, using material both from original documents and from modern historians. The more recent volumes, however, are designed in response to the changing trends in history examinations at 18 plus, most of which now demand the study of documentary sources and the testing of historical skills. Each volume therefore concentrates on a particular topic within a narrower span of time. It consists of eight sections, each dealing with a major theme in depth, illustrated by extracts drawn from primary sources. The series intends partly to provide experience for those pupils who are required to answer questions on documentary material at A-level, and partly to provide pupils of all abilities with a digestible and interesting collection of source material, which will extend the normal textbook approach.

This book is designed essentially for the pupil's own personal use. The author's introduction will put the period as a whole into perspective, highlighting the central issues, main controversies, available source material and recent developments. Although it is clearly not our intention to replace the traditional textbook, each section will carry its own brief introduction, which will set the documents into context. A wide variety of source material has been used in order to give the pupils the maximum amount of experience – letters, speeches, newspapers, memoirs, diaries, official papers, Acts of Parliament, Minute Books, accounts, local documents, family papers, etc. The questions vary in difficulty, but aim throughout to compel the pupil to think in depth by the use of unfamiliar material. Historical knowledge and understanding will be tested, as well as basic comprehension. Pupils will also be encouraged by the questions to assess the reliability of evidence, to recognise bias and emotional prejudice, to reconcile conflicting accounts and to extract the essential from the irrelevant. Some questions, *marked with an asterisk*, require knowledge outside the immediate extract and are intended for further research or discussion, based on the pupil's general knowledge of the period. Finally, we hope that students using this material will learn something of the nature of historical inquiry and the role of the historian.

John Wroughton

Acknowledgements

The author and publisher wish to thank the following who have kindly given permission for the use of extracts from copyright material:
Edward Arnold Ltd – J. Hardman (ed.), *The French Revolution* (1981); Bell & Hyman Ltd – L. W. Cowie, *Eighteenth-Century Europe* (1963); Basil Blackwell Ltd – J. M. Thompson, *Letters of Napoleon*, and *Napoleon Bonaparte: His Rise and Fall* (1958); Blaisdell Ltd – J. H. Robinson, *Readings in European History* (1906); Caldar & Boyars Inc. – Princess E. R. Dashkova, *Memoirs*, trans. and ed. Kyril Fitzlyon (1958); Cambridge University Press – A. Young, *Travels in France During the Years 1787, 1788 and 1789*, ed. C. Maxwell (1950), W. F. Reddaway, *Documents of Catherine the Great* (1931), J. M. Creed and Boys Smith, *Religious Thought in the Eighteenth Century*, *The New Cambridge Modern History* (1934); Jonathan Cape Ltd – P. Doyle, *A History of Political Thought* (1963), P. Geyl, *Napoleon: For and Against* (1958); Le Club Français du Livre – D. Diderot, *Oeuvres complètes* (1973); Librairie Armand Colin, Paris – A. Bayet and F. Albert, *Les Ecrivains Politiques du XVIIIe siècle* (1926); Cornell University Press – F. E. Manuel, *The Age of Reason*; J. M. Dent Ltd – Lord Chesterfield, *Letters to his Son* (1929), Thomas Hobbes, *Leviathan* (1937), *The Social Contract and Discourses by Jean-Jacques Rousseau*, trans. G. D. H. Cole (1938), and F. A. M. Mignet, *History of the French Revolution from 1789 to 1814* (1915); English University Press – R. Charques, *A Short History of Russia* (1959); Eyre-Methuen Ltd – *English Historical Documents*, Vol. VIII, ed. A. Browning (1953); Eyre & Spottiswoode Ltd – S. K. Padover, *The Revolutionary Emperor* (1934); Fontana Paperbacks Ltd – G. Best, *War and Society in Revolutionary Europe 1770–1870* (1982), G. Rudé, *Paris and London in the Eighteenth Century* (1970); *French Historical Studies* – H. T. Parker, 'Napoleon Reconsidered' (1987); Librairie Grund – A. de Vigny, *Servitudes et Grandeur Militaires*; Hamish Hamilton Ltd – A. J. P. Taylor, *The Habsburg Monarchy 1809–1918* (1948); Hamlyn Ltd – N. Harris, *Struggle for Supremacy* (1969); Rupert Hart-Davis Ltd – D. J. Goodspeed, *Bayonets at St Cloud* (1965); Hodder & Stoughton Ltd – I. Grey, *Catherine the Great* (1961); Hollis & Carter Ltd – P. Hazard, *European Thought in the Eighteenth Century*, trans. J. Lewis May (1965); Longmans, Green Ltd – G. P. Gooch, *Frederick the Great* (1947), D. Hume, *Essays Moral, Political and Literary*, eds T. H. Green and T. H. Grose; Macmillan Ltd – H. H. Rowen, *From*

Absolutism to Revolution, C. A. Macartney (ed.), *The Hapsburg and Hohenzollern Dynasties in the 17th and 18th Centuries* (1970), R. C. Bridges, P. Dukes, J. D. Hargreaves and W. Scott (eds), *Nations and Empires* (1969); Methuen Ltd – H. Butterfield, *Select Documents of European History* (1931); Oxford University Press – *Letters Written in Wartime*, ed. H. Wragg (1915), G. N. Clark, *The Seventeenth Century*, 2nd edn (1947), H. Bettenson (ed.), *Documents of the Christian Church* (1943), M. Howard, *War in European History* (1967), A. de Tocqueville, *L'Ancien Régime* (English trans., 1937), and Carl von Clausewitz, *On War*, ed. and trans. Michael Howard and Peter Paret (1976); Paladin Ltd – A. Cobban, *Aspects of the French Revolution* (1968); Pan Books Ltd – John Bowle, *A History of Europe* (1979); Penguin Books Ltd – G. R. Cragg, *The Church and the Age of Reason 1648–1789* (1960), R. J. Forbes and E. J. Dijksterhuis, *A History of Science and Technology* (1963), A. R. Vidler, *The Church in an Age of Revolution 1789–1960* (1961), E. N. Williams, *The Ancien Régime in Europe* (1972), C. Seignobos, *Histoire sincere de la nation française* (1944), *The Memoirs of Chateaubriand*, ed. and trans. R. Baldrick (1965); Peregrine Books/Penguin Ltd – J. L. Talmon, *The Origins of Totalitarian Democracy* (1952); Princeton University Press – R. R. Palmer, *The Age of Democratic Revolution* (1959–64), Peter Putnam, *Seven Britons in Imperial Russia 1698–1812* (1952); Routledge & Kegan Paul Ltd – J. Haller, *The Epochs of German History* (1930); Time-Life International – P. Gay, *Age of Enlightenment* (1966); Ward, Lock Ltd – T. Carlyle, *The French Revolution*; Ward, Lock Educational Ltd – Simon Eliot and Beverley Stern (eds), *The Age of Enlightenment*, vol. II (1979); Weidenfeld & Nicolson Ltd – E. J. Hobsbawm, *The Age of Revolution 1789–1848* (1962); Oswald Wolff Ltd – Ludwig Reiners, *Frederick the Great*, trans. L. P. R. Wigeon (1960).

Every effort has been made to trace all the copyright holders but if any have been inadvertently overlooked the publishers will be pleased to make the necessary arrangement at the first opportunity.

Europe in the Eighteenth Century

The division of European history into chronological periods must always be arbitrary. Some historians have suggested that the eighteenth century does not form a suitable period and would substitute for it one covering the years between the Treaty of Westphalia in 1648 and the outbreak of the French Revolution in 1789. The eighteenth century does, however, remain a convenient period, and it has been usual to regard it as beginning with the death of King Louis XIV in 1715 and ending with the defeat of the Emperor Napoleon in 1815, that is, from the years following the Treaty of Utrecht to those culminating in the Vienna Settlement. It starts and finishes with the frustration of attempts to dominate Europe by France, the leading power of the continent. Between these events lie the developments which led to the French Revolution and its aftermath. The period is important also for the movements known as the scientific revolution and the Enlightenment, which make it in many ways the harbinger of modern times.

It is impossible in this book to have a collection of extracts which covers every aspect of the century. The selection here aims at being representative without vainly attempting comprehensiveness by illustrating its main topics and important features.

It has also been necessary to avoid duplicating documents in this book with those contained in the author's *The French Revolution* in this series. This has affected to some extent sections II, V and VI in this book, but primarily and inevitably it has influenced the contents of section IX. Here it has been necessary to adopt a different approach compared with the other book, which (as does the whole series) only contains extracts from contemporary documents, so that the two books will complement each other and provide a fuller treatment of both the century and the Revolution than would be possible in a single volume.

Historians have paid a great deal of attention to the scientific revolution and the Enlightenment. The first stage of the scientific revolution had already been achieved by the beginning of the eighteenth century with the appearance of Newton's *Principia* in 1687. The Enlightenment as it developed in France sought to translate the scientific discoveries of the previous century into a new outlook and a fresh world-view. Herbert Butterfield considered in *The Origins of Modern Science, 1300–1800* (1950), 'It is important to note that the great movement of the eighteenth century was a literary one – it was not the new discoveries of science in that epoch but, rather, the French *philosophe* movement that decided the next turn of the story and determined the course Western civilization was to take.'

The *philosophes* believed that they could bring into being a novel age in which there would be no tyranny of privilege, censorship or persecution, torture or subjection, and they gained increasing success in changing the ethic of Western civilisation. Their great weakness, however, was as J. S. Mill observed, that they 'anathematized all that had been going on in Europe from Constantine . . . to Voltaire'. They could not think rightly about the present because they did not do justice to the past. Their admiration for science led them into abstract, generalising thought. They put forward theoretical reconstructions of human institutions, such as those of Montesquieu and Rousseau (pp 8, 13 below), but they accepted without question the assumptions upon which these were based – such as that human nature is essentially good, that man would be free and happy if he lived in accordance with his natural instincts, and that he had been corrupted solely by his institutions. The realisation that these could be made the subject of systematic investigation had to await the revolution in historical thinking of the nineteenth century.

While the existence of the Enlightenment is generally accepted, though its nature and scope are much discussed, some historians in this century have asked whether there was such a thing as Enlightened Despotism? They have argued that the 'despots' were really continuing the policy of increasing the power of their states and giving them the necessary fiscal and administrative systems and that their enlightened pretensions were mere self-advertisement. More recently, however, there has been a readiness to recognise the genuineness of the aims of these rulers and the value of their achievements, particularly in promoting education, ameliorating serfdom and establishing religious toleration. One reason for this is that, despite the importance of the three leading Enlightened Despots, historians have realised that it extended beyond them (p 38 below); and the suggestion has been made that a better name for it would be 'enlightened government'.

The eighteenth century saw a decline in the power of the Church in Europe. There were several reasons for this. Though the Enlightenment in Germany and Italy was religious rather than secular, the *philosophes* regarded religion as a superstition and wanted the abolition of the power of the priests with their miraculous pretensions. The Enlightened Despots set out to undermine the entrenched position of the Roman Catholic Church in their dominions. Above all, the subordination of the Church to the State continued in this century under successive governments. In

France, for instance, neither the revolutionaries nor Napoleon would countenance the idea of ecclesiastical independence. Here and in other countries, the Church lost political power which even the religious revival of the next century was not to restore to it.

Throughout these changes, the eighteenth century was still marked by the continuance of the political and cultural dominance of France, which had been established in the previous century. Its international supremacy, however, had already been weakened through its defeat in the War of the Spanish Succession (1701–13). And behind the impressive regime bequeathed to France during the reign of Louis XIV (1643–1715) existed grave and continual weaknesses, which found expression in internal disunity, social discontent and intractable financial problems. The perpetual inability of the royal treasury to raise an adequate annual revenue for the kingdom was worsened by the cost of the wars in which France was engaged throughout the century. France suffered defeat in these wars because it was unable both to maintain its European position and establish an overseas empire. Britain gained possession of the French colonies in the Seven Years War (1756–63), and France's revengeful intervention on the side of the revolting colonists in the American War of Independence (1775–83) brought the financial crisis to a climax.

The outbreak of the French Revolution was expected by many, including the Younger Pitt in England, to eliminate France from international affairs and bring about a period of peace in Europe, but the accompanying resurgence of French nationalism took the republican and imperial armies across the continent, bringing new ideas and political arrangements inexorably into the occupied countries. At the same time, national feeling in these countries themselves was aroused by French rule and contributed to the eventual defeat of their conqueror.

The century ended with a peace settlement that, though it bequeathed Europe a century without a major war, was to face stress and change through the steadily mounting force of this nationalism. It ended also with the defeated Napoleon exiled upon St Helena and creating an image of himself that was to find acceptance in his country and yet lose it that military supremacy which it had tried hard to maintain.

I The Enlightenment

Introduction

When Lord Balfour stated that the eighteenth century began 'for the purpose respectively of science, philosophy and theology' with the publication of Newton's *Principia* (1687), Locke's *An Essay Concerning Human Understanding* (1690) and Toland's deistical work *Christianity Not Mysterious* (1696), he was expressing a long-held view which identified the Enlightenment completely with that of the *philosophes*, which was English in origin, but became increasingly French as the years progressed. Nowadays, however, such a coherent and limited conception of this movement is no longer held. In particular, the importance of the Enlightenment in Germany and Italy is thought to have been underestimated. Johann Gottfried von Heider of Germany and Grambattista Vico of Italy have been seen to express an originality and penetration in their thought which make it clear that France did not monopolise the intellectual life of this century.

Nevertheless, as M. S. Anderson has said in *Historians and Eighteenth-Century Europe, 1715–1789* (1979), 'France's position as the centre of the Enlightenment, the country in which its questions, its doubts and contradictions were sharpest, is beyond challenge' because she was notably 'the leader of eighteenth-century Europe in the generation and spread of ideas', and 'in the physical sciences and in political and social speculation she was pre-eminent, even though her pre-eminence was based on the other side of the Channel by Newton and Locke.'

In his *Essay Concerning Human Understanding*, Locke set out to discover what problems the human mind is able and not able to consider. One of his conclusions was that everything in the human mind is derived from experience, since there are no inborn ideas. This respect for fact and experience strongly influenced Voltaire and fortified his desire for reform in France. Locke's political philosophy, expressed in his *Two Treatises of Government*, was based upon the principle of the ultimate sovereignty of the governed and had a profound effect upon constitution-making in England, the United States of America and France.

As a controversialist, Voltaire has received more attention in the past than the Baron de Montesquieu, who has, however, been regarded by some as the greatest figure in the history of political ideas since the time of ancient Greece. He made a serious attempt to achieve a comprehensive study of contemporary human society. His greatest work, *De l'Esprit des lois*, recommended a system of government based upon the 'mixed constitution' of Britain, which he admired, and though his understanding of it was not entirely accurate, his conception inspired the critics of the *ancien régime* in France and stimulated the attempts at constitutional monarchy during the Revolution.

The new knowledge was systematised in France in the famous *Encyclopédie*, which was first planned by its publisher as an expanded, translated version of the *Encyclopaedia* of Ephraim Chambers, but under its editor, Denis Diderot, it was transformed with the assistance of sympathetic contributors into a work of twenty-eight volumes published in Paris and (later) Amsterdam, which was an exposition of the sceptical, rationalist attitude of the *philosophes*, though in a skilful, elliptical way. Much of it was written, however, by middle-class men, who were liberal and monarchist in their outlook, who do not seem to have wished to destroy the *ancien régime*.

Rousseau stands apart from the other figures of the Enlightenment in France. He came from a lower social class and had been a vagabond in his early life. In his *Du Contrat Social* he concerned himself with the need to free the individual from repressive government because 'man is born free, but everywhere is in chains.' He put forward the theory that the individual should surrender his natural rights, not to any sovereign but to the community under the direction of the general will, an idea which other writers had considered, and since the individual obtains in exchange, so to speak, an inseparable part of the whole common sovereign power, he really is as free as he was before entering into the social contract. His ideas inevitably demolished the foundations of the French monarchy, but his writings were little read before 1789. Only when the Revolution began were they important in providing ideas which supported it. Perhaps the greatest problem facing him, which he never resolved, was that experienced by other political writers – how was the general will to be transferred into the realm of actual popular government?

1 John Locke (1632–4)

(a) The theory of knowledge

For, first, it is evident that all children and idiots have not the least apprehension or thought of them [i.e. innate principles in the mind]; and the want of that is enough to destroy that universal assent which must needs be the necessary concomitant of all innate truths;

it seeming to me near a contradiction to say that there are truths imprinted on the soul which it perceives or understands not; imprinting, if it signify anything, being nothing else but the making of certain truths to be perceived. For to imprint anything on the mind without the mind's perceiving it, seems to me hardly intelligible. If therefore children and idiots have souls, have minds, with those impressions upon them, they must unavoidably perceive them, and necessarily know and assent to these truths; which since they do not, it is evident that there are no such impressions. For if they are not notions naturally imprinted, how can they be innate? And if they are notions imprinted, how can they be unknown? To say a notion is imprinted on the mind, and yet at the same time to say that the mind is ignorant of it, and never yet took notice of it, is to make this impression nothing. No proposition can be said to be in the mind which it never knew, which it was never yet conscious of.

. . .

Let us then, suppose the mind to be, as we say, white paper, void of all characters, without any ideas; how comes it to be furnished? Whence comes it by that vast store which the busy and boundless fancy of man has painted on it with an almost endless variety? Whence has it all the materials of reason and knowledge? To this I answer, in one word, from experience; in that all our knowledge is founded, and from that it ultimately derives itself. Our observation, employed either about external, sensible objects, or about the internal operations of our minds, perceived and reflected on by ourselves, is that which supplies our understandings with all the materials of thinking. These two are the foundations of knowledge, from whence all the ideas we have, or can naturally have, do spring.

John Locke, *An Essay Concerning Human Understanding* (1690), Book I, Chapter II, Section 5, and Book II, Chapter I, Section 2

(b) The dissolution of government

For laws not being made for themselves, but to be by their execution the bonds of society, to keep every part of the body politic in its due place and function, when that totally ceases, the government visibly ceases, and the people become a confused multitude without order or connection. Where there is no longer the administration of justice, for the security of men's rights, nor any remaining power within the community to direct the force, or provide for the necessities of the republic, there certainly is no government itself. . . .

In these, and the like cases, where the government is dissolved, the people are at liberty to provide for themselves, by erecting a new legislature, differing from the other by the change of persons or form or both as they shall find it most for their safety or good. For the society can never by the fault of another lose the nature and original right it has to preserve itself, which can only be done by a settled legislature and a fair and impartial execution of the laws made by it.

John Locke, *Second Treatise of Government* (1690), Chapter XIX, Sections 219 and 220

(c) Voltaire (1694–1778) on Locke

Many a philosopher has written the tale of the soul's adventures, but now a sage has appeared who has, more modestly, written its history. . . . Locke has developed human reason before men, as an excellent anatomist unfolds the mechanism of the human body. Aided everywhere by the torch of physics, he dares to affirm, but he also dares to doubt. Instead of collecting in one sweeping definition what we do not know, he explores by degrees what we desire to know. He takes a child at the moment of its birth, step by step he follows the progress of its understanding; he sees what it has in common with the beasts, and wherein it is set above them; he is guided throughout by the testimony that is in himself, conscious of his own thought.

F. M. A. de Voltaire, *Lettres philosophiques* (1734), ed. F. A. Taylor (1946), pp. 39–41

(d) The importance of Locke

Locke's doctrines . . . became an accepted orthodoxy in England in the eighteenth century, one of the periods in which English thought exercised its greatest influence abroad. He was the main ancestor of all the individualistic liberalism typical of the eighteenth century in England, France and America, and one of the forerunners of the various schools of liberal thought in still more modern times. His influence was partly due to his habit of writing with little response to preceding speculation, and with an easy assumption that no previous knowledge was needed to understand his arguments. None the less he did hold together, if somewhat loosely, the principal threads of the liberal thought of the century of which he saw the end. He convinced the world that the purpose of government was the public good. He established the respectability of tolerance and of revolution in moderate measure.

G. N. Clark, *The Seventeenth Century* (2nd edn, 1947), p 232

Questions

a How do extracts *a* and *c* indicate Locke's purpose in inquiring into 'the origin, certainty and extent of human knowledge?'
b What did Locke consider were man's natural rights in politics?
c Did Locke's conception of the 'social contract' make 'revolution in a moderate measure' respectable?
* *d* 'When Locke's ideas reached first Europe, then America, they looked much more revolutionary than they had done at home' (Stuart Andrews). Discuss this statement.

2 Montesquieu (1689–1755)

(a) The nature of liberty

It is true that in democracies the people seem to do as they wish; but political liberty does not consist in doing as one wishes. In a state, that is to say in a society where there are laws, it can consist only in the power of doing what we ought to desire.
5   We ought to bear in mind what is independence and what is liberty. Liberty is the right to do everything that the laws allow; and if a citizen could do what they forbid, he would no longer possess liberty, because everyone else would have the same power.
Baron de Montesquieu, *De l'esprit des lois* (1748), Book XI, Chapter III

(b) The separation of powers

There are in every state, three sorts of powers: the legislative
10 power, the executive power in matters upon which the rights of the people depend, and the executive power in those upon which justice depends.
By the first, the prince or magistrate makes laws, temporary or permanent, and amends or abrogates those which are made. By
15 the second, he makes peace or wages war, sends or receives embassies, maintains public order, prevents invasions. By the third, he punishes crimes or judges disputes between individuals. This last is called the judicial power, and the other simply the executive power of the state. . . .
20 There is no liberty if the legislative power is combined with the executive power in the same body or the same body of magistrates because there is fear that the same monarch or the same senate may make tyrannical laws and enforce them tyrannically.
Similarly, there is no liberty if the judicial power is not separated

from the legislative and executive powers. If it is combined with the legislative power, the power over the life and liberty of the citizens will be arbitrary, because the judge will also be the legislator. If it is combined with the executive power, the judge will have the force of an oppressor.

All would be lost, if the same man, or the same body of notables, or of nobles or of the people, exercised these three powers, that of making laws, that of executing public resolutions and that of judging crimes or disputes between individuals.

Ibid., Book XI, Chapter VI

(c) The British constitution

Since, in a free state, every man who is considered to have an independent opinion ought to be governed by himself, it would be necessary for the people in a body to have the legislative power; but, since this is impossible in large states, and has many disadvantages in small ones, the people must do through their representatives everything they cannot do by themselves. . . .

There are always in a state people distinguished by birth, wealth or honours; but if they were mingled with the people, and if they had only one voice like the others, the common liberty would become their slavery, and they would have no interest in defending it, because most of the resolutions would be directed against them. The part which they have in legislation must therefore be proportionate to the other advantages they possess in the state. This would be secured if they form a body which has the right to check the projects of the people, in the same way as the people have the right to check theirs.

Thus, the legislative power will be entrusted both to the body of nobles and to the body which will be chosen to represent the people, who will each have their separate assemblies and debates, as well as their separate outlook and interests. . . .

The executive power must be in the hands of a monarch, because that part of government, which almost always requires immediate action, is better administered by one than by several; while that which depends on the legislative power is often better managed by several than by an individual.

Ibid., Book XI, Chapter VI

(d) The comparison with the French constitution

Montesquieu could not tolerate the absolute autocracy of France, but lauded with high praise the mixed constitution of Great Britain, which to him with the cursory glance of a stranger appeared to have achieved the correct equilibrium between the innumerable environmental conditions. He admired especially in the English constitution what he considered to be the complete separation of the legislature and executive. He saw in such a separation a formidable check on the development of an absolutist government resulting from the fusion of all powers into an individual control centre. The English constitution had the merit in his eyes of being capable of adaptation without violent upheaval. Nothing was so rigid in that it could not be modified gradually and without a jar that would shatter the whole structure to pieces. The French constitution on the contrary was inflexible, absolutist and contrary to nature, for it could not adapt itself to the changing needs of the community.

Phyllis Doyle, *A History of Political Thought* (1963), p 205

Questions

a Does extract *a* suggest whether Montesquieu placed the greater importance upon liberty or public safety?
b How did Montesquieu develop in extract *b* Locke's ideas about arbitrary government?
c What did Montesquieu consider in extract *c* was the part taken by the Crown, the House of Lords and the House of Commons in the government of Britain?
* d 'He believed that France's salvation lay in undoing the evil work of Richelieu and Louis XIV and returning to the old monarchy of Henry IV or Louis XII.' Consider this description of Montesquieu's outlook.

3 Diderot (1713–84) and the *Encyclopédie* (1771–72)

(a) Eagle

The eagle is a bird sacred to Jupiter, from the day when this god, having consulted the augurs in the island of Naxos on the success of the war he was about to undertake against the Titans, beheld an eagle which was a good omen. It is said also that the eagle fed him on ambrosia during his childhood, and it was to recompense him for this care that he placed it among the stars. The eagle is to be seen in pictures of Jupiter, sometimes at the god's feet, sometimes at his side and almost always carrying thunderbolts in its claws. There is much in this to suggest that the whole fable is based upon observation of the flight of the eagle, which loves to raise itself into the highest clouds and to dwell in the region of thunder. This is sufficient to make the eagle the bird of the god of the heavens and the air and to give him thunder to wield. The pagans were simply led by their imagination when they came to honour their gods; superstition would rather suppose the most extravagant and ridiculous visions than to have none. These visions are then consecrated by time and popular credulity; and woe to him who, without having been called by God to the great and perilous task of a missionary, cares so little for his own tranquillity and knows so little of men, as to devote himself to teaching them. If you cast a ray of light into a nest of owls, you will only dazzle their eyes and arouse their cries. A hundred times happier are people whose religion invites them only to believe things that are true, sublime and holy and to imitate only virtuous actions; such is our religion in which the philosopher has only to follow his reason to come to the foot of our altars.

Denis Diderot, *Oeuvres complètes* (Le Club Français du Livre, 15 vols, 1973), XV, pp 43–4

(b) Irreligion

An irreligious man is one who is without religion, lacks respect for sacred things and has no belief in God, and who regards piety and the other virtues, which belong to his creed, as meaningless words.

One is only irreligious in the society of which one is a member; it is certain that it is no crime for a Moslem to neglect the law of Mohammed in Paris, nor for a Christian to forget his religion in Constantinople.

It is not so with moral principles; they are the same everywhere. Neglect of these is blameworthy in all places and all times. People are divided into different creeds, religious or irreligious, according to the part of the surface of the earth to which they travel or where they live; morality is the same everywhere.

It is the universal law which the finger of God has written on the hearts of everyone.

It is an eternal precept based upon universal understanding and necessity.

It is essential therefore not to confuse immorality and irreligion. Morality may exist without religion; and religion may even exist with immorality.

Without extending his gaze beyond this life, there are many reasons, all well considered, which can show a man that to be happy in this world there is nothing better to do than to be virtuous.

It does not need insight or experience to realize that there is no vice that does not bring with it some degree of unhappiness, and no virtue that is not accompanied by some measure of good fortune; that it is impossible that the wicked man can be entirely happy and

the good man completely unhappy; and that, despire momentary
55 interests and attractions, this is still the only course to follow.
    Ibid., pp 313–14

(c) Prayer

To pray is to ask for a thing which one considers a favour from someone who consequently can refuse it without injustice. To pray when one has the right to demand is to suspect or accuse to whom one prays of injustice; it is often to demean oneself. One prays to
60 God, to the king, to one's mistress and to a friend. The principle of prayer is that of power on one side and of necessity on the other.

One prays a man to dishonour himself either in his eyes or in the eyes of others when the thing for which one prays to him is unseasonable, unjust, illegal or dishonest.
    Ibid., p 366

(d) Resurrection

65 Resurrection is to return to life. Jesus Christ raises Lazarus from the dead. He himself was raised from the dead. There are resurrections in all the religions of the world; but only those of Christianity are true; all the others, without exception, are false.
    Ibid., p 366

(e) The condemnation of the Encyclopédie, 1752

7 February 1752 – The King, having had report made to him
70 concerning what has happened on the subject of a work entitled Encyclopaedia or Explanatory Dictionary of the Sciences, Arts and Crafts, written by a group of men of letters (two volumes of this work having as yet been printed), H.M. has realized that in these two volumes there has been inserted several maxims tending to the
75 destruction of the royal authority, the establishment of a spirit of independence and revolt, and the fostering, by obscure and equivocal phrases, of error, corrupt morals, irreligion and unbelief. H.M., always attentive to anything which concerns public order and the honour of religion, has judged proper to interpose his authority to
80 check the evils which might follow from the pernicious maxims scattered about this work; and to this effect, the report having been read, the King, being in his council, has ordered and does order with the advice of the Chancellor, that the first two volumes of the work entitled Encyclopaedia or Explanatory Dictionary of the
85 Sciences, Arts and Crafts, by a group of men of letters, shall be

and shall remain suppressed. It is expressly prohibited and forbidden to all printers, publishers and others, to reprint or have reprinted the said two volumes; as also to sell or in any way distribute the printed volumes which they still possess, on pain of a fine of 1,000 livres, or of such other penalty as shall be deemed necessary – even, if printers and publishers are concerned, the penalty of forfeiture and deprivation of their licence. The present order shall be read and published, and shall be placarded wherever necessary.

F. A. Isambert, *Recueil général des anciennes lois françaises* (29 vols, 1822–33), XXII, pp 250–1, in H. Butterfield (ed.), *Select Documents of European History*, 1931, pp 52–3

Questions

a   How does the surface meaning of extracts *a* and *d* differ from the intended meaning?
b   What provoking examples of the meaning of 'prayer' are given in extract *c*?
c   What 'obscure and equivocal phrases', as condemned in extract *e*, can be found in the extracts from the *Encyclopédie*?
* d   Do you agree that, though Diderot was not a systematic thinker, he nevertheless had the most profoundly original mind among the *philosophes*?

4   Jean-Jacques Rousseau (1712–78)

(a) A forerunner: Thomas Hobbes (1588–1679)

The agreement . . . of men is by Covenant only, which is Artificiall: and therefore it is no wonder if there be somewhat else required (besides Covenant) to make their Agreement constant and lasting; which is a Common Power, to keep them in awe, and to direct their actions to the Common Benefit.

The only way to erect such a Common Power, as may be able to defend them from the invasion of Forraigners, and the injuries of one another, and thereby to secure them in such sort, as that by their own industrie, and by the fruites of the Earth, they may nourish themselves and live contentedly; is, to conferre all their power and strength upon one Man, or upon an Assembly of men, that they may reduce all their Wills, by plurality of voices, unto one Will: which is as much as to say, to appoint one Man, or Assembly of men, to beare their Person; and every one to owne, and to acknowledge himself to be Author of whatsoever he that so beareth their Person shall Act, or cause to be Acted, in those things which concerne the Common Peace and Safetie; and therein to submit their Wills, every one to his Will, and their Judgements, to his Judgement. This more than Consent, or Concord; it is a reall Unitie of them all, in one and the same Person, made by Covenant of every man with every man. . . . This done, the Multitude so united in one Person, is called a COMMON-WEALTH, in latine CIVITAS. This is the generation of that great LEVIATHAN (to speak more reverently) of that *Mortall God*, to which we owe under the Immortall God, our peace and defence.

Thomas Hobbes, *Leviathan* (Everyman edition, 1937), p 89

(b) The social compact

If then we discard from the social compact what is not of its essence, we shall find that it reduces itself to the following terms –

'*Each of us puts his person and all his power in common under the supreme direction of the general will, and, in our corporate capacity, we receive each member as an indivisible part of the whole.*'

At once, in place of the individual personality of each contracting party, this act of association creates a moral and collective body composed of as many members as the assembly contains votes, and receiving from this act its unity, its common identity, its life and its will.

The Social Contract and Discourses by Jean-Jacques Rousseau, trans. G. D. H. Cole (Everyman edition, 1938), p 15

(c) Forced to be free

In order then that the social compact may not be an empty formula, it tacitly includes the undertaking, which alone can give force to the rest, that whoever refuses to obey the general will shall be compelled to do so by the whole body. This means nothing less than that he will be forced to be free; for this is the condition which, by giving each citizen to his country, secures him against all personal dependence. In this lies the key to the working of the political machine; this alone legitimises civil undertakings, which, without it, would be absurd, tyrannical and liable to the most frightful abuses.

Ibid., p 18

(d) The moral importance of the social bond

The passage from the state of nature to the civil state produces a very remarkable change in man, by substituting justice for instinct in his conduct, and giving his actions the morality they had formerly lacked. Then only, when the force of duty takes the place of

50 physical impulses, and right of appetite, does man, who so far had considered only himself, find that he is forced to act on different principles, and to consult his reason before listening to his inclinations. Although, in this state, he deprives himself of some advantages which he got from nature, he gains in return others so
55 great, his faculties are so stimulated and developed, his ideas so extended, his feelings so enobled, and his whole soul uplifted, that, that did not the abuses of this new condition often degrade him below that which he left, he would be bound to bless continually the happy moment which took him from it for ever, and instead
60 of being a stupid and unimaginable animal, made him an intelligent being and a man.
      Ibid., pp 18–19

Questions

  a Do you agree that 'the "general will" of Rousseau is Hobbes's Leviathan with his head chopped off?'
  b Did Rousseau succeed in combining the sovereignty of the State with the freedom of the subject?
  c Does extract *d* justify Rousseau's contention in extract *c* that coercion is in accordance with the individual's general will?
* *d* How did Rousseau destroy the intellectual and moral bases of the *ancien régime* in France?

II   Church and State

Introduction

Among the ways in which the authority of the Church was challenged during the eighteenth century, the threat in the intellectual sphere was very serious. John Locke's exploration of the working of the human mind and his emphasis upon fact and reason (p 5 above) was influential, particularly upon the development of Deism, though he himself objected to the title of 'Deist'. Deism accepted belief in the existence of God, but not in revealed religion. John Toland insisted upon the supremacy of reason to which both revelation and the supernatural had to be subordinated. The scepticism of David Hume, the greatest of British philosophers, opposed all previously accepted certainties, including belief in miracles, as shown in the ironic concluding passage of his Essay (p 18 below). By reducing reason to a product of human experience, he destroyed its claim to be supremely conclusive as the *philosophes* insisted, and, indeed, as he himself was aware, he destroyed all real knowledge.

Such religious fervour as existed in the early eighteenth century was attracted towards Jansenism, a religious system originating with the teaching of Cornelius Jansen (1585–1638), Bishop of Ypres, based on the doctrines of St Augustine, which emphasised human corruption and divine election in much the same way as Calvinism had done. It was most influential in France, where after papal condemnation and persecution, some of its followers degenerated into extravagant fanaticism. Its power, however, was not destroyed, and in France and other countries, notably the Netherlands and Tuscany, it supported the attacks made upon the Roman Catholic Church.

In France the Jansenists supported especially the Gallicans in the Parlement of Paris, who maintained the right of the French Church to be free in certain respects from papal control, against the Ultramontanes, who insisted upon the absolute authority of the Pope in matters of faith, morals and discipline. The Gallican cause was reinforced by the *philosophes*, whose attitude towards the relationship of Church and State was expressed by Voltaire (p 21 below). Its greatest victory was the condemnation of the Jesuits in 1762 by the Parlement, which compelled Louis XV two years later to issue an edict forbidding their work in France. And in 1773 Pope Clement XIV dissolved the Society.

Another threat to the Church came from Enlightened Despotism. Its effect was twofold – the rulers curtailed its powers and privileges and promoted religious toleration. Frederick II of Prussia, sceptical of all dogmas, was assisted by the Lutheran tradition of obedience to the State, but he also relied upon the diminishing authority of the Papacy in international affairs. In the Habsburg lands, the Empress Maria Theresa's piety caused tension with her son, Joseph II, who was himself a sincere Christian, but determined on reforms which he believed had a religious justification.

Napoleon was indifferent to religion, but he realised its political importance and wanted to end the disunity which the Revolution had caused in France by its attack upon Roman Catholicism. For this reason he made the Concordat of 1801 with the Pope, but followed it by the Organic Articles, which restrained considerably the Papacy's powers in France. His relations with it were further strained by his treatment of the Church in his conquered territories, of which the decree abolishing the Spanish inquisition and monastic orders was typical (p 27 below), and his annexation of the Papal States in Italy.

1 Religious Dissidence

(a) *The doctrines of the Gospel not contrary to reason*

After having said so much of *Reason*, I need not operosely shew what it is to be contrary to it; for I take it to be very intelligible from the precedent Section, *that what is evidently repugnant to clear and distinct Ideas, or to our common Notions, is contrary to Reason*: I go on therefore to prove, that *the Doctrines of the Gospel*, if it be the word of God, *cannot be so*. But if it be objected, that very few maintain they are: I reply that no *Christian* I know of (for we shall not distract the Ashes of the Dead) expressly says *Reason* and the *Gospel* are contrary to one another. But, which returns to the same, very many affirm, that though the Doctrines of the latter cannot in themselves be contradictory to the Principles of the former, as proceeding both from God; yet, that according to our Conceptions of them, *they may seem directly to clash*: And that though we cannot reconcile them by reason of our corrupt and limited Understandings; yet from the Authority of *Divine Revelation*, we are bound to believe and acquiese in them; or as the *Fathers* taught'em to speak, *to adore what we cannot comprehend*.

This famous and admirable Doctrine is the undoubted Source of all *Absurdities* that ever were seriously vented among Christians.

20 Without the Pretence of it, we should never hear of the *Transubstantiation*, and other ridiculous Fables of the Church of *Rome*; nor of any of the *Eastern Ordures*, almost all receiv'd into the Western Sink: Nor should we be ever banter'd with the *Lutheran Impanation*, or the *Ubiquity* it has produc'd, as one Monster ordinarily begets
25 another. And tho the *Socinians* disown this Practice, I am mistaken if either they or the *Arians* can make their Notion of a *dignif'd and Creature God capable of Divine Worship*, appear more reasonable than the Extravagences of other Sects touching the Article of the Trinity. . . .
    John Toland, *Christianity not Mysterious* (1696), in J. M. Creed and Boys Smith, *Religious Thought in the Eighteenth Century* (1934), p 256

(b) Miracles and faith

30 So that, upon the whole, we may conclude, that the Christian Religion not only was at first attended with miracles, but even at this day cannot be believed by any reasonable person without one. Mere reason is insufficient to convince us of its veracity: And whoever is moved by Faith to assent to it, is conscious of a
35 continued miracle in his own person, which subverts all the principles of his understanding, and gives him a determination to believe what is most contrary to custom and experience.
    David Hume, 'Essay of Miracles', *Essays Moral, Political and Literary*, ed. T. H. Green and T. H. Grose (2 vols, 1898), II, p 108

(c) Jansenism: the 'Five Propositions', 1653

  1 Some commandments of God to men wishing and striving to be righteous are impossible with regard to the present strength that
40 they possess; and they lack the grace by which they may become possible.
  2 Interior grace is never resisted in the state of fallen nature.
  3 For merit or demerit in the state of fallen nature freedom from necessity is not required in man but freedom from compulsion.
45   4 Semipelagians admit the necessity of prevenient interior grace for single acts, even for the beginning of faith; and they are heretics in this, that they wish grace to be of such a kind as human will can resist or obey.
  5 It is Semipelagian to say that Christ died and shed his blood
50 for all men.
    Innocent X, *Cum occasione*, 1653, in Henry Bettenson (ed.), *Documents of the Christian Church* (1943), p 376

(d) The Jansenist convulsionaries

A suburb resounded with acclamations: the remains of one of the elect there accomplished, in a single day, more wonders than Jesus Christ did in all his life. Everyone ran there; I was in the crowd. I had hardly arrived when I heard the cry: miracle! miracle! I approached, I looked, and I saw a lame boy walking with the help of three or four kindly persons who supported him; and the people, who were amazed, repeated: miracle! miracle! Where then was the miracle, foolish people? Did you not see that this imposture was only a change of crutches? The miracles on this occasion were just as it always is with ghosts. I am convinced that all those who have seen ghosts, believed in them already, and that those who saw the miracles there were firmly resolved to see them.

Denis Diderot, *Oeuvres complètes*, eds J. Assezat and M. Tourneaux (20 vols, 1875–7), LIII (*Pensées philosophiques*, 1746)

Questions

a What religious attitude towards reason is criticised by Toland in extract *a*?
b What did Hume really mean by his remarks about miracles in extract *b*?
c Does the Pope's statement in extract *c* that the Jansenists, like former heretics, denied that 'Christ died and shed his blood for all men' explain why Diderot called them 'the elect' in extract *d*?
★ *d* Why was the intellectual outlook of the Enlightenment hostile to contemporary Christianity?

2 Ecclesiastical Affairs in France

(a) The Gallican Declaration, 1632

Many people are striving to overthrow the decrees of the Gallican Church . . . and to destroy the foundation of the liberties, which are based on the sacred canons and on the tradition of the Fathers; others, under the pretext of defending them, have the audacity to attack the supremacy of St Peter and his successors the Popes of Rome. . . . The heretics, for their part, are doing their utmost to make this power which keeps the peace of the Church, intolerable to kings and peoples. . . .

Wishing to remedy this state of affairs. . . .

Article I. . . . We declare that Kings and Sovereigns are not, by God's command, subject to any ecclesiastical power in temporal matters; that they cannot be deposed, directly or indirectly, by the authority of the heads of the Church; that their subjects cannot be dispensed from obedience, nor absolved from the oath of allegiance. . . .

Article II [The plenitude of power in spiritual matters possessed by St Peter and his successors, none the less remains, as laid down by the decrees of the Council of Constance].

Article III Thus the use of the apostolic power must be regulated, by following the canons made by the Holy Spirit and sanctified by universal reverence. The rules, customs and constitutions accepted in the realm and Church of France must have their strength and virtue . . . since the greatness of the Holy See requires that the laws and customs established with its consent and that of the Churches remain invariable.

Article IV Although the Pope has the chief voice in questions of faith, and his decrees apply to all churches and to each particular church, yet his decision is not unalterable unless that the consent of the Church is given.

Article V [These maxims sent to all the French bishops and churches that they may be unanimous].

> W. F. Reddaway, *Select Documents of European History 1492–1715* (1930), p 267

(b) Ultramontane doctrines

Your Majesty understands the consequences of such principles which desire no less than to authorise all the undertakings of the Roman Court, to make the ecclesiastical power sovereign in your kingdom, to give it a temporal authority independent of yours – principles which, claiming to establish decrees as laws of the State, would give it, so to speak, your crown and make it the absolute judge of the liberty, possessions, honour and life of your subjects. That, Sire, your Parliament cannot ignore without betraying the loyalty which we owe to Your Majesty.

Our fathers always considered, and we still consider after them, not only that the ecclesiastical power cannot attach itself to any direct or indirect rights over the temporality of our kings, since they acknowledge no superior on earth; but they always believed concerning ecclesiastical matters that, far from the authority of our kings being regarded as irrelevant or impotent, consideration and approval by that royal authority was always requisite and necessary.

> *Remonstrance du Parlement de Paris*, 7 April 1737, in Albert Bayet and François Albert, *Les Ecrivains politiques du XVIIIe siècle* (1926), pp 408–9

(c) Voltaire on Church and State (1)

We have instituted priests in order that they alone may do as they should – be moral teachers of our children. These teachers should be paid and respected, but they should not claim to possess jurisdiction, supervision and privileges; they should not in any case make themselves the equal of the magistrate. An ecclesiastical assembly, which presumes to make a citizen kneel before it, plays the role of a schoolmaster who corrects his children or a tyrant who punishes his slaves.

It is an insult to reason and the law to pronounce these words: *civil and ecclesiastical government*. One should say: *civil government and ecclesiastical regulations*, and none of these regulations should be imposed except by the civil power.

F. M. A. de Voltaire, *Idées Républicaines*, in ibid., p 117

(d) Voltaire on Church and State (2)

No law made by the Church should ever have the least force unless expressly sanctioned by the government. It was owing to this precaution that Athens and Rome escaped all religious quarrels.

Such religious quarrels are the trait of barbarous nations or such as have become barbarous.

The civil magistrate alone may permit or prohibit labour on religious festivals, since it is not the function of the priest to forbid men to cultivate their fields.

Everything relating to marriage should depend entirely upon the civil magistrate. The priests should confine themselves to the august function of blessing the union.

Lending money at interest should be regulated entirely by the civil law, since trade is governed by civil law.

All ecclesiastics should be subject in every case to the civil government, since they are subjects of the state.

Never should the ridiculous and shameful custom be maintained of paying to a foreign priest the first year's revenue of land given to a priest by his fellow-citizens [annates to the Pope].

No priest can deprive a citizen of the least of his rights on the ground that the citizen is a sinner, since the priest – himself a sinner – should pray for other sinners, not judge them.

Officials, labourers and priests should all alike pay the taxes of the state, since they all alike belong to the state.

F. M. A. de Voltaire, *Dictionnaire philosophique portatif* (1765), sub. '*Lois civiles et ecclésiastiques*', in J. H. Robinson, *Readings in European History* (2 vols, 1906), II, pp 380–1

(e) The condemnation of the Jesuits, 1762

The said Court [the Parlement of Paris], assembled in all its Chambers, doing justice upon the said appeal alleging corrupt practice, lodged by the Attorney-General for the Crown, concerning the Rules and constitutions of the Society calling itself of Jesus . . . declares that there is corrupt practice in the said Rule of the Society calling itself of Jesus in its bulls, briefs, letters apostolic, constitutions, declarations on the said constitutions, forms of vows, decrees of the generals and general congregations of the said Society called '*oracles of the living voice*', and generally in all the rules of the said Society or actions of a similar nature, in all that constitutes the essence of the said Rule. Declares the said Rule inadmissable by its nature in any civilised State, as contrary to natural right, derogatory to all temporal and spiritual authority, and tending to introduce into Church and State, under the specious pretence of a religious Rule, not an order which truly and solely aspires towards evangelical perfection, but rather a political body, whose distinguishing mark lies in a continual endeavour to attain by all means, direct or indirect, underhand or open, at first complete independence and then the usurpation of all authority. . . .

F. A. Isambart, op. cit., XXII, pp 322ff.

Questions

a   What do extracts *a* and *b* indicate were the main differences between Gallicanism and Ultramontanism?
b   What did Voltaire consider should be the position and purpose of the Church in France?
c   What do you understand by the phrases 'oracles of the living voice' (line 91) and 'contrary to natural right' (line 94) in extract *e*?
★ d   Why did the Jesuits meet with widespread hostility during the eighteenth century?

3   Enlightened Despotism and Religion

(a) Frederick II of Prussia (1)

Frederick pressed to its logical conclusion the view that the civil ruler has absolute power over all forms of religious activity. The Church possessed no independent rights. . . . Frederick granted equal toleration to all faiths, partly because he regarded all of them as equally spurious, partly because military considerations made it expedient. But toleration did not extend to unlimited attacks on religion; faith might be a delusion, but it was still a valuable instrument of social control, and anything that kept the masses quiet was too useful to be discarded. Infidelity was the prerogative

of the elite. The restricted freedom which Frederick permitted the Church rested on a utilitarian motive; contempt for Christianity as a faith was modified by appreciation of the Church as an instrument.
G. G. Cragg, *The Church and the Age of Reason 1648–1789* (1960), p 96

(b) Frederick II of Prussia (2)

I am neutral between Rome and Geneva. If Rome seeks to encroach upon Geneva, Rome gets the worst of it; if Geneva seeks to oppress Rome, Geneva is condemned. In this way . . . I try to unite them by reminding them that they are all fellow-citizens, and that no one can like a man who wears a red costume as much as another who wears a grey one. I try to maintain friendly relations with the Pope.

. . .

The Pope is an old neglected idol in his niche. He is at present the chief almoner of Kings. His thunderbolts are no more. His policy is known. Instead of laying peoples under an interdict and deposing sovereigns as of old, he is content if no one deposes him and lets him say mass quietly in St Peter's.
Frederick II, *Political Testament* (1752), *Die Politischen Testamente Friedrich's des Grossen*, ed. G. B. Volz (1920), in G. P. Gooch, *Frederick the Great* (1947), p 284

(c) Maria Theresa

Letter to Joseph, late July 1777 – Nothing is so necessary and salutary as religion. Will you allow everyone to fashion his own religion as he pleases? . . . The result will be the rule of the stronger and more unhappy times like those which we have already seen. A manifesto by you to this effect can produce the utmost distress and make you responsible for many thousands of souls. And what are my own sufferings, when I see you entangled in opinions so erroneous? What is at stake is not only the welfare of the State but your own salvation, that of a son who since his birth has been the purpose of all my actions, the salvation of your soul. Turning your eyes and ears everywhere, mingling your spirit of contradiction with the simultaneous desire to create something, you are ruining yourself and dragging the monarchy down with you into the abyss, destroying the fruits of all the laborious care of your forefathers, who at the cost of the greatest pains bequeathed these lands to us and even greatly improved their condition because they introduced our holy religion into them, not, like our enemies, with violence and cruelty, but with care, pains and expense. No spirit of persecution, but still less any spirit of indifference or tolerantism [sic]; in this I hope to maintain myself so long as I live, and I only wish to live so long as I can hope to descend to my ancestors with the consolation that my son will be as great, as religious, as his forebears, that he will return from his erroneous views, from those wicked books whose authors parade their cleverness at the expense of all that is most holy and most worthy of respect in the world, who want to introduce an imaginary freedom which can never exist and which degenerates into licence and into complete revolution.

C. A. Macartney (ed.), *The Hapsburg and Hohenzollern Dynasties in the 17th and 18th Centuries* (1970), p 267

(d) Joseph II (1)

Being convinced, on the one hand, that all violence to conscience is harmful, and, on the other, of the great benefit to religion and to the State from a true Christian tolerance, We have found Ourselves moved to grant to the adherents of the Lutheran and Calvinist religions, and also to the Non-Uniat Greek religion, everywhere, the appropriate practice of their faith, regardless of whether it had been previously customary or introduced, or not. The Catholic religion alone shall continue to enjoy the prerogative of the public practice of its faith, but members of the two Protestant religions and the existing Non-Uniat Greek shall be permitted the private practice thereof in any place where . . . the said non-Catholics do not already enjoy the right of practising it publicly.

The Toleration Patent (October 1781) in ibid., p 347

(e) Joseph II (2)

A General Seminary is to be established, which is to be the common training centre of instruction for all future secular clergy and religious. At it all the young men are to complete the entire course of public instruction in theology, after which they are to spend a year in all kinds of practical pastoral ministrations under the supervision of the Seminary staff.

The Seminaries Patent (March 1783) in ibid., p 349

(f) Joseph II (3)

70   1   Where the parochial clergy are too few in numbers, or too far from the communes which they serve, either, according to the numbers of the populations, new priests or local curates shall be appointed, or the districts lying too far from their place of worship shall be transferred to other parishes, the principle to be followed
75   being that in future no person shall have to journey more than an hour to his place of worship.

2   Where there is a shortage of churches and vicarages, these, unless built voluntarily by the manorial authority, shall be constructed out of the Religious Fund.

The Livings Patent (October 1783) in ibid., p 343

Questions

a   Compare the attitude of Frederick II, Maria Theresa and Joseph II towards religious toleration.
b   What is the meaning of the phrases 'secular clergy', 'religious', 'pastoral ministrations' and 'parochial clergy'?
c   What similarity of motive on the part of Joseph II can be found in extracts *e* and *f*?
* d   'Turning your eyes and ears everywhere, mingling your spirit of contradiction with the simultaneous desire to create something' (Maria Theresa). Is this an accurate description of Joseph II's religious policy?

4   Napoleon and the Church

(a) 'The Mystery of Religion'

The mystery is not that of the Incarnation. I do not discuss that, any more than the other dogmas of the Church. But I see in religion the whole mystery of Society. I hold . . . that apart from the precepts and doctrines of the Gospel, there is no society that can
5   flourish, nor any real civilisation. What is it that makes the poor man take it for granted that ten chimneys smoke in my palace while he dies of cold – that I have ten changes of raiment in my wardrobe while he is naked – that on my table at each meal there is enough to sustain a family for a week? It is religion which says
10   to him that in another life I shall be his equal, indeed that he has a better chance of being happy there than I have.

Paul Droulers, *Action pastorale et problèmes sociaux sous la Monarchie de Juillet* (1954), p 117, in A. R. Vidler, *The Church in an Age of Revolution 1789–1960* (1961), p 19

(b) The Concordat, 1801

The government of the French Republic recognises that the Catholic, Apostolic and Roman religion is the religion of the great majority of French citizens. His Holiness equally recognises that this same religion has secured and still now expects the greatest glory and good from the establishment of Catholic worship in France, and the special profession which the Consuls of the Republic are making.

Therefore, following this mutual recognition, both for the good of religion and the maintenance of internal tranquillity, they have agreed on the following:

1 The Catholic, Apostolic and Roman religion will be freely exercised in France. Its worship will be public, in conformity with the police regulations which the government still consider necessary for public tranquillity.

2 The Holy See, in concert with the government, will make a new arrangement of the French dioceses.

3 His Holiness will declare to the holders of titles to French bishoprics that he confidently expects them, for the sake of peace and unity, to make any sacrifice, even that of their sees. After this exhortation, if they refuse to make this sacrifice for the good of the Church (though His Holiness does not expect a refusal), the government of the bishoprics governed by the new arrangement shall be provided in the following manner.

4 The First Consul of the Republic, within three months after the publication of the Bull of His Holiness, will name the archbishops and bishops under the new arrangement. His Holiness will confer canonical institution in the form established in France before the change of government.

6 Before taking office, the bishops shall swear the following oath to the First Consul in person. . . .

'I swear and promise before God, upon the holy Gospel, to show obedience and fidelity to the government established by the constitution of the French Republic. I promise also to have no part nor lot in any counsel nor connection with any league, at home or abroad, which is contrary to public tranquillity; and if, in my diocese or elsewhere, I learn of any conspiracy to the prejudice of the State, I will see that the government knows of it.'

13 His Holiness, for the sake of peace and the happy re-establishment of the Catholic religion, declares that neither he nor his successors will disturb in any way those who have acquired the alienated ecclesiastical lands, and that in consequence, possession of these lands, with the rights and revenues attached to them, shall remain permanently in the hands of these purchasers or of those with legal right to them.

14 The government promises suitable payment to bishops and

priests whose dioceses and parishes are comprised under the new arrangement.
> E. Reich, *Select Documents Illustrating Medieval and Modern History* (1905), pp 448–52

(c) The organic articles, 1801

1 No bull, brief, rescript, decree, mandate, provision or document serving as a provision, nor any other communication from the Court of Rome, even though it may concern only private individuals, shall be received, published, printed or otherwise put into execution without government authorisation.

No individual calling himself nuncio, legate, vicar or apostolic commissioner, or availing himself of any other title, may carry out any office in connection with the affairs of the Gallican Church, whether he do it on French soil or elsewhere, unless he has the same authorisation.

3 The decrees of foreign synods, and even of general councils, may not be published in France until the government has examined their form and found out whether they are consistent with the laws, rights and franchises of the French Republic and has satisfied itself that their publication will not in any way injure or affect the public peace.

4 No national or provincial council, no diocesan synod, no deliberating assembly, shall take place without the express permission of the government.

> G. F. de Martens, *Recueil des principaux Traités – Supplement* 4 vols, 1802–8), II, p 531, in H. Butterfield, op. cit., pp 80–1

(d) Abolition of the Inquisition and monastic orders in Spain

Madrid, 4 December 1808 – The tribunal of the Inquisition is abolished, as inconsistent with the civil sovereignty and authority. The property of the Inquistion shall be sequestered and fall to the Spanish state, to serve as security for the bonded debt.

Considering that the members of the various monastic orders have increased to an unusual degree and that, although a certain number of them are useful in assisting the ministers of the altar in the administration of the sacraments, the existence of too great a number interferes with the prosperity of the State, we have decreed and do decree as follows:

The number of convents now in existence in Spain shall be reduced to a third of their present number. This reduction shall be

90 accomplished by uniting the members of several convents of the same order into one. From the publication of the present decree, no one shall be admitted to the novitiate or permitted to take the monastic vow until the number of the religious of both sexes has been reduced to one third of that now in existence. . . . All regular
95 ecclesiastics, who desire to renounce the monastic life and live as secular ecclesiastics, are at liberty to leave their monasteries. . . .

Correspondance de Napoleon Ier (32 vols, 1858–69), XVIII, nos 14, 526–7, in J. H. Robinson, op. cit., II, p 512

(e) The annexation of the Papal States, 1809

Napoleon, Emperor of the French, King of Italy, Protector of the Confederation of the Rhine, etc., in consideration of the fact that when Charlemagne, Emperor of the French and our august
100 predecessor, granted several countries to the Bishops of Rome, he ceded these only as fiefs and for the good his empire; further, that since this association of spiritual and temporal authority has been, and still is, a source of dissensions, and has but too often led the pontiffs to employ the influence of the former to maintain the
105 pretensions of the latter, and thus the spiritual concerns and heavenly interests, which are unchanging, have been confused with terrestrial affairs, which by their nature alter according to circumstances and the policy of the time; and since all our proposals for reconciling the security of our armies, the tranquillity and the
110 welfare of our people, and the dignity and integrity of our empire, with the temporal pretensions of the popes, have failed, we have decreed and do decree what follows:

1 The Papal States are reunited to the French Republic.

2 The city of Rome, so famous by reason of the great memories
115 which cluster about it and as the first seat of Christianity, is proclaimed a free imperial city.

Corresp. Nap. Ier., XIX, nos 15, 219, in ibid., p 513

Questions

a   Was Napoleon's religious policy in agreement with the ideas of the *philosophes* about the part the Church should play in society?
b   Why did the Concordat require the nomination of a new hierarchy in the French Church?
c   Explain the meaning of 'bull' (line 36), 'Holy See' (line 26), 'synod' (line 69) and 'novitiate' (line 92).
*   d   How far did Napoleon's annexation of the Papal States eventually contribute towards his downfall?

III The Scientific Revolution

Introduction

'The so-called scientific revolution,' Herbert Butterfield wrote, 'outshines everything since the rise of Christianity and reduces the Renaissance and Reformation to the rank of mere episodes, mere internal displacements within the system of medieval Christendom.' By the beginning of the eighteenth century, the progress of the new science had taken place largely through the work of the members of the scientific societies founded during the previous century of which the most important were the *Académie des Sciences* of Paris and the Royal Society of London. Its operation was most prominent in mathematics and physics, and it made important practical contributions to astronomy and navigation.

The seal was set upon the work of these scientists by Sir Isaac Newton (1642–1747), whose discovery of the principle of universal grativation provided a complete and coherent system of dynamics, the branch of physics which treats of matter and motion, where the nature of a moving body and the cause of its motion are both considered. He himself stated that he 'subjected the phenomena of nature to the laws of mathematics' to give 'a clear and positive meaning' to the universal order of the heavens. The whole universe seemed to be subject to one unifying system of law. The effects of the Newtonian synthesis were taken beyond the realm of physical science in the eighteenth century into the world of nature.

Indeed, this became the almost exclusive object of scientific attention throughout the century, and the desire to discover, through systematic investigation, a coherent world order led to the investigation and classification of animals and plants. Prominent among the naturalists who undertook this was the Comte de Buffon (1707–88), of whom an admirer once said, 'He loves order and makes it everywhere', a quality he demonstrated by suggesting that all animals had originally a common ancestor. His *Natural History* of fifteen volumes set out to contain all the known facts of the subject.

At the same time, technology received encouragement from the Enlightenment. One of the purposes of the *Encyclopédie* was to provide detailed articles on trades and mechnanical processes. This was part of the general attack on the outlook and values of the *ancien régime* since the culture of the court established by Louis XIV at Versailles was predominantly and narrowly literary and aesthetic. Diderot's article on 'Art' (p 35 below) was published in the periodical *Mercure de France* in advance of the first volume of the *Encyclopédie*, which aroused interest in its scope. Early in the Revolution, the National Assembly adopted the metric system of weights and measures to facilitate science and technology, which by then was having an effect on industry. Though France made industrial advances, Britain entered the new age of the Industrial Revolution at least half a century before other countries, the effect of which was seen when Napoleon sought to deprive Europe of British goods through his Continental System.

1   Sir Isaac Newton (1642–1727)

(a) The law of universal gravitation

Hitherto we have explained the phenomena of the heavens and of our sea by the power of gravity, but we have not yet assigned the cause of this power. This is certain, that it must proceed from a cause that penetrates to the very centre of the sun and planets,
5   without suffering the least diminution of its force; that operates not according to the quantity of the surfaces of the particles upon which it acts (as mechnanical causes use to do), but according to the quantity of the solid matter which they contain, and propagates its virtue on all sides to immense distances, decreasing always as
10 the inverse square of the distances. . . .

But hitherto I have not been able to discover the cause of this property of gravity from phenomena, and I frame no hypotheses; for whatever is not deducted from the phenomena is to be called a hypothesis; and hypotheses, whether metaphysical or physical,
15 whether of occult qualities or mechanical, have no place in experimental philosophy. In this philosophy particular propositions are inferred from the phenomena, and afterward rendered general by induction. Thus it was that the impenetrability, the mobility, and the impulsive force of bodies, and the laws of motion and of
20 gravitation, were discovered. And to us it is enough that gravity does really exist, and acts according to the laws which we have explained, and abundantly serves to account for all the motions of the celestial bodies, and of our sea.

And now we might add something concerning a most subtle
25 spirit which pervades and lies hid in all gross bodies; by the force and action of which spirit the particles of the bodies attract one another at near distances and cohere, if contiguous; and electric bodies operate to greater distances, as well repelling as attracting the neighbouring corpuscles; and light is emitted, reflected, refracted,
30 inflected, and heats bodies; and all sensation is excited, and the

members of animal bodies move at the command of the will, namely, by the vibration of this spirit, mutually propagated along the solid filaments of the nerves, from the outward organs of sense to the brain, and from the brain to the muscles. But these are things that cannot be explained in few words, nor are we furnished with that sufficiency of experiments which is required to an accurate determination and demonstration of the laws by which this electric and elastic spirit operates.

Isaac Newton, *Philosophie Naturalis Principia Mathematica-Scholium Generale* (1687), in R. J. Forbes and E. J. Dijksterhuis, *A History of Science and Technology* (2 vols, 1963), I, pp 241–2

(b) Voltaire on Newton

I have taught you, may Sir Isaac rejoin, that all bodies gravitate towards one another in proportion to their quantity of matter; that these central forces alone keep the planets and comets in their orbits, and cause them to move in the proportion before set down. I demonstrate to you, that it is impossible there should be any other cause which keeps the planets in their orbits, than that general phenomenon of gravity. For heavy bodies fall on the earth according to the proportion demonstrated of central forces; and the planets finishing their course according to the same proportions, in case there were another power that acted upon all these bodies, it would either increase their velocity, or change their direction. Now not one of these bodies ever has a single degree of motion or velocity, or has any direction but what is demonstrated to be the effect of the central forces; consequently it is impossible there should be any other principle.

Give me leave once more to introduce Sir Isaac speaking: shall he not be allowed to say, My case and that of the ancients is very different? These saw, for instance, water ascend in pumps, and said, the water rises because it abhors a *vacuum*. But with regard to myself, I am in the case of a man who should have first observed that water ascends in pumps, but should leave others to explain the cause of this effect. The anatomist who first declared, that the motion of my arm is owing to the contraction of my muscles, taught mankind an indisputable truth; but are they less obliged to him because he did not know the reason why the muscles contract? The cause of the elasticity of the air is unknown, but he who first discovered this spring performed a very signal service to natural philosophy. The spring that I discovered was more hidden and universal, and for that very reason mankind ought to thank me the more. I have discovered a new property of matter, one of the secrets of the Creator; and have calculated and discovered the effects of it. After this shall people quarrel with me about the name I give it?

Vortices may be called an occult quality because their existence was never proved: attraction on the contrary is a real thing, because its effects are demonstrated, and the proportions of it are calculated. The cause of this cause is among the arcana of the Almighty.

>F. M. A. de Voltaire, *Letters Concerning the English Nation* (Glasgow, 1759), Letter XVI, pp 94–5

(c) Newton and the Enlightenment

These two consequences of Newton's work – confidence in the scientific method and modesty about man's capacity to know – appear at first to be contradictory. But they do come together, and it is precisely where they join that the energy for the Enlightenment arose. Newtonian thought meant, first of all, that only patient and sceptical inquiry could produce reliable results. The vaulting philosophical systems of seventeenth-century metaphysicians, and the improbable tales of saints and miracle-workers, were equally suspect and equally useless.

Secondly, Newtonian thought meant that the scientific method could, with care, be applied to non-scientific disciplines – to theology, history, morals. Thirdly, Newtonian thought meant that men did not have to concern themselves with airy fantasies about first causes, but could instead concentrate their intellectual energies on practical problems, on improving man's lot in the world. . . .

Admiring the immense prestige that science had acquired, they [the *philosophes*] took the scientific attitude for their own. With science as a licence they proceeded to examine all men's assertions on all fields of knowledge with critical freedom. They also took it as a philosophical position wholly incompatible with divine revelation. . . . All of them believed that when science advanced, religion had to retreat. Thus the uneasy peace between reason and revelation became war, and the Scientific Revolution was turned into an open rebellion against the faith that had governed Europe for more than a thousand years.

>Peter Gay, *Age of Enlightenment* (1966), p 20

(d) Science and the French Revolution

Let us never forget that long before we did, the sciences and philosophy fought against the tyrants. Their constant efforts have made the revolution. As free and grateful men, we ought to establish them among us and cherish them for ever. For the sciences

and philosophy will maintain the liberty which we have conquered.
A member of the National Convention, quoted in E. J.
Hobsbawm, *The Age of Revolution 1789–1848* (1962), p 327

Questions

a To what extent do extracts *a* and *b* express the aspects of Newtonian thought described in extract *c*?
b What is the meaning of the phrases 'occult quality' and 'the arcana of the Almighty'?
c Why did the speaker in extract *d* claim that 'the sciences and philosophy fought against the tyrants'?
★ *d* How far is it true that Newton gave the age of the Enlightenment its belief in the power and scope of human reason?

2 The Comte de Buffon (1707–88)

(a) Scientific discipline and hope

Let us continue to add to our experience and avoid all theorizing, at least until we have mastered the facts. We shall find out easily enough some day where to put our material, and even if we are not lucky enough to complete the building, we shall at least have the satisfaction of knowing that our foundations have been well and truly laid. And perhaps – who knows? – we may have progressed beyond all our expectations with the superstructure.

Comte de Buffon, Preface to his translation of Hale's *La statique des végétaux* (1735), in Paul Hazard, *European Thought in the Eighteenth Century* (trans. Lewis May, 1965), p 159

(b) His view of geology

The changes which the earth has undergone during the last two or three thousand years are inconsiderable, compared with the great revolutions which must have happened in those ages that immediately succeeded the creation. For, as terrestrial substances could only acquire solidity by the continual action of gravity, it is easy to demonstrate, that the surface of the earth was at first much softer than it is now; and, consequently, that the same causes, which at present produce but slight and almost imperceptible alterations during the course of many centuries, were then capable of producing very great revolutions in a few years. It appears, indeed, to be an incontrovertible fact, that the dry land which we now inhabit, and even the summits of the highest mountains, were formerly covered with the waters of the sea; for shells, and other marine bodies, are still found upon the very tops of mountains. It likewise appears, that the waters of the sea have remained for a long track of years upon the surface of the earth; because, in many places, such immense banks of shells have been discovered, that it is impossible so great a multitude of animals could exist at the same time. This circumstance seems likewise to prove, that, although the materials on the surface of the earth were then soft and, of course, easily disunited, moved, and transported, by the waters; yet these transportations could not be suddenly effected. They must have been gradual and successive, as sea-bodies are sometimes found more than one thousand feet below the surface. Such a thickness of earth or of stone could not be accumulated in a short period. Although it should be supposed, that, at the deluge, all the shells were transported from the bottom of the ocean, and deposited upon the dry land; yet, beside the difficulty of establishing this supposition, it is clear, that, as shells are found incorporated in marble, and in the rocks of the highest mountains, we must likewise suppose, that all these marbles and rocks were formed at the same time, and at the very instant when the deluge took place; and, that, before this grand revolution, there were neither mountains, nor marbles, nor rocks, nor clays, nor matter of any kind, similar to what we are now acquainted with, as they all, with few exceptions, contain shells, and other productions of the ocean. Besides, at the time of the universal deluge, the earth must have acquired a considerable degree of solidity, by the action of gravity for more than sixteen centuries. During the short time the deluge lasted, therefore, it is impossible that the waters should have overturned and dissolved the whole surface of the earth, to the greatest depths that mankind have been able to penetrate.

Comte de Buffon, *Histoire naturelle générale et particulière* (15 vols, 1749–67), I, *Second Discours: Histoire et théorie de la terre*, in Simon Eliot and Beverley Stern (eds), *The Age of Enlightenment* (2 vols, 1979), II, pp 196–7

(c) Man and the animals

From what has been advanced, the following general conclusions may be drawn: that man is the only animated being on whom Nature has bestowed sufficient strength, genius and ductility, to enable him to subsist and multiply in every climate of the earth. No other animal, it is evident, has obtained this great privilege; for, instead of multiplying everywhere, most of them are limited to certain climates, and even to particular countries. Man is totally a production of heaven: but the animals, in many respects, are creatures of the earth only. Those of one continent are not found in another; or, if there are a few exceptions, the animals are so changed and contracted that they are hardly to be recognised. Is any further argument necessary to convince us, that the model of their form is not unalterable; that their nature, less fixed than that of man, may be varied, and even absolutely changed in a succession of ages; that, for the same reason, the least perfect, the least active, and the worst defended, as well as the most delicate and heavy species, have already, or will soon disappear; for their very existence depends on the form which man gives or allows to the surface of the earth? The prodigious *mammoth*, whose enormous bones I have often viewed with astonishment, and which were, at least, six times larger than those of the largest elephant, has now no existence; yet the remains of him have been found in many places remote from each of other, as in Ireland, Siberia, Louisiana, etc. The species was unquestionably the largest and strongest of all quadrupeds, and since it has disappeared, how many smaller, weaker and less remarkable species must likewise have perished without leaving any evidence of their past existence? How many others have undergone such changes, either from degeneration or improvement, occasioned by the great vicissitudes of the earth and waters, the neglect or cultivation of Nature, the continued influence of favourable or hostile climates, that they are now no longer the same creatures? Yet the quadrupeds, next man, are beings whose nature and form are the most permanent. Birds and fishes are subject to greater variations: the insect tribes are liable to still greater vicissitudes: and, if we descend to vegetables, which ought not to be excluded from animated Nature, our wonder will be excited by the quickness and facility with which they assume new forms.

        Comte de Buffon, ibid., vol IX, '*Histoire naturelle des quadrupeds*', in ibid., II, pp 234–5

Questions

  a Do you consider that Buffon was guided in extracts *b* and *c* by the principles set out in extract *a*?
  b What is the 'universal deluge' to which Buffon refers in line 44?
  c What is there to suggest in extracts *b* and *c* why Buffon aroused the hostility of orthodox Christians of his time?
* *d* What were the reasons for the beginning of the study of nature as a systematic pursuit in the eighteenth century?

3 Technological Advance

(a) The value of research

Should we assume that we will not find anything if we add our efforts to the whims of chance and introduce order and method into our research? If we now possess secrets which men formerly did not hope to uncover, and if we may conjecture from the experience of the past, why should the future not hold riches for us that we can scarcely count on to-day? If, a few centuries ago, anyone had said to those people who measure possibilities by the reach of their genius and do not imagine anything beyond what they already know, that there exists a dust that breaks rocks and overthrows the thickest walls from an unbelievable distance, that a few pounds of this dust, enclosed in the depths of the earth, shake the earth, make their way through the enormous mass that covers them, and open up an abyss large enough to contain an entire city, these people would certainly have compared such effects to the action of wheels, pulleys, levers, counterweights, and other known machines; they would have declared that such a dust is a mere figment of the imagination and that only lightning, or the cause that produces earthquakes by means of an inimitable mechanism, can produce such fearful prodigies. . . . How much enormous speculation would have occasioned by the project of raising water by fire, as was carried out for the first time in London, especially if the inventor of the machine would have modestly presented himself as a man little versed in mechanics? If this were the only attitude towards invention nothing either great or small would be produced. Men who render hasty judgments upon inventions that do not deviate from established practice and sometimes are merely slight modifications of familiar machines, requiring at most a skilful worker to carry them out, men, I repeat, who are so narrow-minded that they judge these inventions to be impossible, should know that they themselves are not learned enough to formulate appropriate aspirations.

The Encyclopaedia (Vol I, 1751), Article 'Art' by Diderot, in Eliot and Stern, op cit, II, p 148

(b) A French ironworks

Messrs Espivent had the goodness to attend me in a water expedition, to view the establishment of Mr Wilkinson, for boring cannon, in an island in the Loire below Nantes. Until that well-known English manufacturer arrived, the French knew nothing of the art of casting cannon solid, and then boring them. Mr Wilkinson's machinery, for boring four cannons, is now at work, moved by tide wheels, but they have erected a steam engine, with a new apparatus for boring more; M de la Motte, who has the direction of the whole, showed us a model of this engine, about six feet long, five high, and four or five broad; which he worked for us, by making a small fire under the boiler that is not bigger

than a large tea kettle; one of the best machines for a travelling philosopher that I have seen.
Arthur Young, *Travels in France During the Years 1787, 1788, 1789*, ed. C. Maxwell (1950), p 117

(c) The metric system

Decree of the National Assembly of 8 May 1790 – The National Assembly, wishing to enable the whole of France to benefit forever from the advantage which should result from the uniformity of weights and measures, and desiring that the relationship of the old measures to the new should be clearly determined and understood, decrees that His Majesty should be entreated to give orders to the several departments of the kingdom to the end that they ensure that they receive from everyone of the municipalities included in each department and that they send to Paris, to be remitted to the Secretary of the Academy of Sciences, a perfectly exact standard of the various ordinary weights and measures which are in use there.

It is next decreed that the King shall similarly be entreated to write to His Britannic Majesty and to request him to invite the Parliament of England to co-operate with the National Assembly in establishing a natural unity of weights and measures; that consequently under the auspices of the two nations, delegates from the Academy of Sciences of Paris may be able to meet an equal number of members chosen from the Royal Society of London, in a place which both shall judge most convenient to determine at the latitude of 45 degrees, or any other latitude which may be preferred, the length of the pendulum, and deducing from it an invariable standard for all weights and measures.
E. Reich, *Select Documents*, p 443

Questions

a What did Diderot mean by the 'dust that breaks rocks' (line 9) and the 'project of raising water by fire' (lines 20–1)?
b Do extracts *a* and *c* each represent a rational approach to science and technology?
c What were the origins of the Academy of Sciences and the Royal Society (lines 62–3)?
★ d What hindered the advance of technology in France before the Revolution?

IV   The Enlightened Despots

Introduction

The phrase 'Enlightened Despotism' originated only during the second quarter of the nineteenth century from German historians, who applied it mainly to the internal policies of Frederick the Great, and it has never been defined exactly. Generally, however, it has been taken to mean an attempt to save the old, traditional form of monarchy, which could no longer rely upon the divine sanction hitherto accorded it. The Enlightened Despot was no longer responsible to God, but to his subjects, and he was expected to govern them in accordance with the ideas of the Enlightenment.

The rulers influenced by these ideas governed a considerable number of European countries, large and small, which extended widely across the continent. They included Charles III of Spain, Gustavus III of Sweden and Leopold, Grand Duke of Tuscany, as well as some princes in the German and Italian states and ministers in countries such as Naples, Portugal and Denmark; but the leading Enlightened Despots are usually considered to be Catherine II of Russia, Frederick II of Prussia and Joseph II of Austria (the brother of Leopold of Tuscany).

Historians have long doubted whether Catherine the Great was truly an Enlightened Despot. Her liberalism has often been regarded as a mere hypocritical sham. This common view is expressed in the extract from Richard Charques (p 41 below). Lately, however, some historians have taken a more favourable view of her policy. Thus, the work of the Legislative Commission, set up by her to reform the laws of Russia (p 39 below), has been regarded as offering her empire a system of government which, if maintained by her successors, would have produced a monarchy capable of ruling without despotism and reliance upon military power. And this seems to have been the view of the British Envoy at her court. Again, might not her opposition to the French Revolution, as expressed in her edict of 8 February 1793 imposing an oath upon Frenchmen living in Russia, be explained by fear of the consequences a similar such violent upheaval have brought about in Russia?

Was Frederick the Great really an Enlightened Despot? At one time there would have been no doubt about this. His contemporaries onwards regarded him as the first Enlightened Despot, the supreme model which other rulers sought to imitate. During this century, however, this conception has been criticised. For instance, Walther Hubatsch in *Frederick the Great: Absolutism and Administration* (1975) wrote, 'Frederick was less influenced by the Enlightenment as a guideline for action than by *Raison d'état* interpreted in an enlightened way.' And the Prussian General Code (p 43 below), which preserved the country's social divisions and increased the numbers of the nobility serving in official posts, has been taken as an indication of the way in which he had frequently to temper the realities of state power in relation to his enlightened hopes.

More recently, however, his reputation has been considered more favourable, and emphasis has been placed upon his efforts to revive Prussian agriculture, trade and industry after the losses brought about by the Seven Years War. The extract on p 45 below illustrates such efforts by Frederick. In July 1779, when he was sixty-seven, he visited an area of marshland northwest of Berlin, which had been drained at his expense and settled with three hundred families. He made notes, such as those in this extract, upon the condition of the towns, villages, forest and fields in this new enterprise.

Finally, Joseph II's achievements have undergone a revaluation in comparison with those of his mother, Maria Theresa (p 73 below), but otherwise his reputation has remained more constant that that of the two other leading Enlightened Despots. He is seen, as in his Instructions to his District Commissioners (p 46 below), to be a monarch who used his absolute authority in efforts to make his subjects prosperous and contented. At the same time, he achieved less than either Catherine or Frederick did, whether because of failure in his character and policy or the social and economic structure of his dominions or the unfortunate effect of the approach of the age of revolution in Europe upon his aspirations and efforts. An extract from a letter by the British Minister in Vienna in 1787 relates a conversation by the Emperor on the situation as he found it.

1 Catherine II of Russia

(a) Her Instructions to the Legislative Commission, 1767

Chap. II

13 What is the true End of Monarchy? Not to deprive People of their natural Liberty; but to correct their Activities, in order to attain the *supreme Good*.

14 The Form of Government, therefore, which best attains this
5 End, and at the same Time sets less Bounds than others to natural Liberty, is that which coincides with the Views and Purposes of rational Creatures, and answers the End, upon which we ought to

fix a steadfast Eye in the Regulations of Civil Polity.

15 The Intention and the End of Monarchy, is the Glory of the Citizens, of the State and of the Sovereign.

16 But, from this Glory, a Sense of Liberty arises in a People governed by a Monarch; which may produce in these States as much Energy in transacting the most important Affairs, and may contribute as much to the Happiness of the Subjects, as even Liberty itself.

Chap. VIII

81 The Love of our Country, Shame, and the Dread of publick Censure, are Motives which restrain, and may deter Mankind from the Commission of a Number of Crimes.

82 The greatest Punishment for a bad Action, under a mild Administration, will be for the Party to be convinced of it. The civil Laws will there correct Vice with the more Ease, and will not be under a Necessity of employing more rigorous Means.

83 In these Governments, the Legislature will apply itself more to prevent Crimes, than to punish them, and should take more Care to instil Good Manners into the Minds of the Citizens, by proper Regulations, than to dispirit them by the Terror of corporal and capital Punishments.

84 In a Word, what ever is termed Punishment in the Law is, in Fact, nothing but Pain and Suffering.

85 Experience teaches us, that, in those Countries where Punishments are mild, they operate with the same Efficacy upon the Minds of the Citizens, as the most severe in other Places.

Chap. XI

250 A Society of Citizens, as well as every Thing else, requires a certain fixed Order: There ought to be *some to govern*, and *others to obey*.

251 And this the Origin of every Kind of Subjection; which feels itself more or less alleviated, in Proportion to the Situation of the Subjects.

252 And, consequently, as the Law of Nature commands *Us* to take as much Care, as lies in *Our* Power, of the Prosperity of all the People; we are obliged to alleviate the Situation of the Subjects, as much as sound Reason will permit.

253 And therefore to shun all Occasions of reducing People to a State of Slavery, except the *utmost* Necessity should *inevitably* oblige us to do it; in that Case, it ought not to be done for our Benefit; but for the Interest of the State: Yet even that Case is extremely uncommon.

254 Of whatever Kind Subjection may be, the civil Laws ought to be on guard, and, on the other, against the Dangers which may arise from it.

255 Unhappy is that Government, which is compelled to institute *severe* Laws.
W. F. Reddaway, *Documents of Catherine the Great* (1931), pp 215ff.

(b) Catherine and the French Revolution, 1793

I the undersigned swear before Almighty God and on His Holy Gospel, that I have never actually or freely given any adhesion to the impious and seditious principles that are now being professed in France, and I regard the government that has been established there a usurpation and a violation of all law. I look upon the death of the Most Christian King Louis XVI as an abominably base crime. I am fundamentally convinced of the holiness of the religion that has come down to me from my forefathers, and I fully admit my duty to be faithful and obedient to the King to whom the crown of France has fallen by right of succession. Therefore while I enjoy the sure refuge which Her Imperial Majesty of All the Russias has deigned to allow me within her dominions, I promise to observe the sacred religion in which I was born, and to conduct myself in complete submission to the laws of Her Imperial Majesty. Also I will break off all correspondence with Frenchmen at home, who recognise the monstrous government at present existing in France, and I will not renew it until legitimate authority has been restored, and Her Imperial Majesty has given me express permission. If I act against my present oath, I agree to submit to all the rigour of the law both in this world and the next, and I will bow to the terrible judgment of God. And, as a sign of this oath, I kiss the words of our Lord and the Cross of my Saviour.

K. Waliszewski, *Le roman d'une Imperatrice* (2 vols, 1893), I, p 401, in H. Butterfield, *Select Documents*, pp 50–1

(c) Her enlightenment

Whatever the sentiments she derived from Voltaire, in the dubious way in which she came to the throne Catherine had no choice but to court the favour of the emancipated nobility. The alliance she struck with them left intact all the prerogatives of autocracy, but for their part it enabled the nobility to stretch authority over their peasants to the point at which they themselves were enthroned as local autocrats. . . .

Like other enlightened despots among her contemporaries, the Empress of Russia enjoyed play-acting. Enlightenment in Catherine was, indeed, not much deeper than her vanity; despotism, on the other hand, was implicit in her ambition. Frederick the Great, notoriously shrewd in these matters, described her as very ambitious and very vain. Vanity was only too evident in her profession of advanced opinions, in her tireless correspondence with the great intellectual figures of the day, in her purchase of Diderot's library for the Hermitage palace, in her own versatile but unoriginal authorship. For all her liveliness of mind and astute grasp of affairs Voltaire's 'Semiramis of the North' is above all else an egotist who wishes to be flattered.

Richard Charques, *A Short History of Russia* (1959), pp 109–10

(d) A contemporary British view

At present the Czarina's attention is engaged by a favourite project, the success of which will do her more real honour, and be of greater advantage to her, than the winning of a battle or the acquisition of a kingdom. She, whose penetrating genius is equally happy in discovering defects and finding resources to remedy them, has long beheld with regret the confusion, tediousness, ambiguity and injustice of the laws of her Empire: to correct them has long been the object of her ambition; and for this purpose she has examined and compared with the utmost attention and precision the different legislations of other countries. . . . She has formed a Code of Laws . . . a most noble undertaking and worthy of the ambition of a Great Prince, who prefers the title of legislator to the fame of conquest.

Sir George Macartney, British Envoy in St Petersburg, 1766, *English Historical Documents* ed. A. Browning (1953), VIII, p 459

Questions

a To what extent did Montesquieu's ideas about liberty and the law (p 39 above) influence Catherine's Instructions to the Legislative Commission?
b What were the 'impious and seditious principles now being proposed in France' (line 55)? What is the meaning of the phrase 'Semiramis of the North' (line 92)?
c Do you agree with the view that Catherine preferred 'the title of Legislator to the fame of conquest' (line 105–6)?
★ d Was Catherine a cynical tyrant or a frustrated idealist?

2 Frederick II of Prussia

(a) The Prussian General Code of 1791

Introduction: On the Laws in General

1 This general code contains the provisions by which the rights and obligations of inhabitants of the state, so far as they are not determined by particular laws, are to be judged.

6★ Decrees or other measures of higher authority, which have been issued in contested cases without judicial cognizance, create neither rights nor obligations.

9★ Particular favours, privileges and exceptions to the law, arising from the action of the sovereign, are valid only so far as the particular rights of a third party are not thereby injured.

16 The laws of the state bind all its members without difference of estate, rank or family.

58 Privileges and grants of liberty, in doubtful cases, must be so interpreted as to do the least damage to third parties.

77★ The welfare of the state in general, and of its inhabitants in particular, is the aim of civil society and the general objective of the laws.

79★ The laws and ordinances of the state should restrict the natural liberty and rights of the citizens no further than the general welfare demands.

83 Every inhabitant of the state has the right to demand its protection for his person and property.

84 No man therefore is entitled to obtain his rights by his own powers.

89 The rights of man arise from his birth, from his estate, and from actions and arrangements with which the laws have associated a certain determinate effect.

90 The general rights of man are grounded on the natural ability to seek further his own welfare, without injury to the rights of others.

92 The particular rights and duties of members of the state rest upon the personal relationship in which each stands to the others and to the state itself.

93 Rights which are not supported by the laws are called imperfect, and give no ground for complaints or pleas in court.

94 Actions forbidden by neither natural nor positive law are called permissible.

Part I: Title I
Of Persons and their Rights in General

1 Man is called a person so far as he enjoys certain rights in civil society.

2 Civil society consists of a number of smaller societies and

★ These clauses were printed in 1791, but omitted in 1794.

estates, bound together by Nature or Law, or both.

6 Persons, to whom by their birth, destination, or principal occupation, equal rights are ascribed in civil society, make up together an estate or the state.

7 Members of each estate have, as such, and considered as individuals, certain rights and duties.

9 The rights and duties of various societies in the state are further defined by their relation to each other and to the supreme head of the state.

Part II: Title IX
On the Duties and Rights of the Noble Estate

1 The nobility, as the first estate in the state, most especially bears the obligation, by its distinctive destination, to maintain the defence of the state, both of its honour without and of its constitution within.

21 In regard to the essential rights and attributes of the noble estate, there is no difference between the old and new nobility.

34 Persons of the nobility are normally subject to the jurisdiction only of the highest court in the province.

35 The nobleman has an especial right to places of honour in the state for which he has made himself fit.

36 But the sovereign retains the power to be the judge of fitness and make selection from among candidates.

37 Only the nobleman has the right to possess noble property.

38 Which properties are noble is determined by the particular constitutions of the several provinces.

40 Only the nobleman may create entails and family trusts for noble properties.

41 Noble property-owners have the right to exercise, in their own name, the hunting rights appertaining to their property.

42 They have the jurisdictional powers pertaining to their property exercised in their name.

43 They possess the honorific rights that go with church patronage.

45 They may use the names of their property as personal names, and in official documents or on public occasions, use the possession thereof as a special title.

46 Only the resident nobility normally have the right to appear in the noble assemblies of circles and provinces, and to have a voice on matters under consideration there.

51 Persons of the burgher estate cannot own noble property except by permission of the sovereign.

60 Burgher owners cannot convey ownership of noble property to other persons of burgher estate, except by special concession.

76 Noblemen shall normally engage in no burgher livelihood or occupation.

77 Where a wholesale business is not associated with a gild, a nobleman may enter upon it.

79 No nobleman, normally, except with special permission of the sovereign, may become a member of a closed merchant gild.

80 Particular rights and duties of the nobility, as belonging either to the whole estate, or to individual members, with respect to their person and property, are determined by the special laws and constitutions of the different provinces.

81 Whoever, by concealing or denying his noble estate, slips into a gild or corporation and carries on a burgher trade, will suffer the loss of his noble rights.

82 The same is all the more true when anyone of noble birth chooses a dishonourable way of life, or any way of life by which he sinks into the common people.

Allgemeines Gesetzbuch für die preussischen Staaten (4 vols, 1791), and *Allgemeines Landrecht für die preussischen Staaten* (1794) in R. R. Palmer, *The Age of Democratic Revolution* (2 vols, 1959–64), I, pp 509–12

(b) The well-being of Prussia

On the estates of Graf Wallis they sell their flax to Bohemia; why is it not spun and treated in the County of Glatz? – The town of Striegau complain that they have no manufactures and no source of wealth; I do not see what can be done to help them unless some new manufacture can be started there – the preparation of vitriol or something similar. – The towns of Schweidnitz and Nesse lack roofing tiles; shall have to think about this. – N.B. for the tax-register of Glatz a distinction must be made between the good, worthy nobility and foreigners. – When a farmer emigrates from Glatz his estate is confiscated – Complaints from Schmiedeberg of oppression by merchants; investigate and send me a report. – More sheep could be kept in the Glatz area if they were grazed in woods on the mountains; but question whether their wool would be good or not; at least it would help the poor country people who could live on goats' milk.

Ludwig Reiners, *Frederick the Great* (trans. L. P. R. Wigeon, 1960), p 227.

Questions

a Does it appear that the clauses, which were omitted in 1794 from the Prussian General Code, were treated in this way because of their likeness to French revolutionary ideas?

b Explain the meaning of 'entail' (line 69), 'church patronage' (line 75), 'burgher estate' (line 83) and 'merchant gild' (line 92).

    c What was the economic importance in the eighteenth century of 'flax' and 'vitriol' (lines 103, 107)?
★ *d* 'The most enlightened despot was Frederick II' (Lord Acton). Do you agree with this judgement?

3 Joseph II of Austria

(a) Maria Theresa and Enlightenment

Maria Theresa to Joseph, 24 December 1775 – We both suffer from a great misfortune, with the best will in the world we do not understand one another. Perhaps I am too greatly distressed when you fail to show me that confidence and frankness which I should
5 have thought were due to me; and this turns my days into weariness. It is indeed I who can say that for 36 years I have interested myself only in you. Twenty-six of these have been happy, but I could not say the same just now, for I cannot reconcile myself to principles which are too lax in regard to religion and morals. You make too
10 great a show of your antipathy to all the old customs and all the clergy, and also of your loose principles in matters of morality and conduct. This disturbs me, with good reason, and I am alarmed about your delicate situation; it makes me shudder for the future.

    Alfred Ritter von Arneth, *Geschichte Maria Theresa's* (10 vols, 1863–9), II, p 99, in H. Butterfield, op cit, p 43

(b) Joseph's Instructions to his District Commissioners, 1784

They were to observe:
15   Whether the censual and vital statistics registers were kept.
    Whether the houses were numbered.
    What was the condition of the buildings.
    Whether the population was industrious or lazy; well-to-do or poor; and why.
20   Whether the conscription books were kept in order.
    Whether the barracks were habitable.
    How many men could be quartered among citizens and peasants.
    Whether the army behaved properly towards the civilian population.
25   Whether the population had sufficient protection.
    Whether the toleration edicts were observed.
    Whether there was any superstition.
    Whether the clergy were respected, and what their discipline was.
30   Whether the divine services were properly carried out and whether the churches were in good condition.
    Whether the preachers delivered indiscreet sermons.

Whether anyone cared for the orphans, foundlings and homeless children.
Whether anything was being done for the blind, deaf and crippled children to make them ultimately self-supporting.
What was the condition of the schools.
Whether there were any roving clowns and jugglers on the land.
Whether the restrictions against drunkenness were carried out.
Whether there was a need for more workhouses and prisons.
Whether the laws were carried out.
Whether the judges were obedient to the superior courts.
Whether the roads were cleared.
Whether there were sufficient precautions in the sale of poisons.
Whether the sale of contraceptive methods was prohibited.
Whether the Church penances and the dishonouring punishments of unfortunate girls were abolished, and whether there were institutions for the saving of such girls, and foundlings.

S. K. Padover, *The Revolutionary Emperor* (1934), pp 186–7

(c) Joseph on his difficulties

3 August 1787 – 'His Britannic Majesty knows by his own experience, that it is the unhappy lot of monarchs to see their upright intentions frequently misapprehended, and their principles calumniated. . . . I have lately seen my subjects in the Netherlands on the very brink of open rebellion from the frantic adoption of views which have been artfully and incessantly instilled into their minds by designing lawyers, bigoted priests, and a few men of higher birth, who are new-fangled dabblers in what *they* call patriotism. The feebleness of my government in the Low Countries had, by timid and unwarrantable concessions, in a manner encouraged the arrogant demands of my subjects, and by yielding a ready consent to every encroachment on my rights the governors at length left to the Flemish leaders no other difficulty save that of *inventing* new pretensions. The only excuse those governors offered for their conduct was the solemn asseveration, repeated in every despatch, that *this*, and *this*, and *this*, must be conceded; otherwise the Low Countries would be inevitably and irrevocably lost to the House of Austria. *I* never felt that danger; I never foresaw and still less confirmed the concessions which, being granted by persons invested with no sort of authority to relinquish any of the rights of sovereignty, are in themselves *null and void*. The steps I have already taken have in some degree opened the eyes of the Flemish nation, and I trust I shall be able to bring them back to reason and justice. . . .'

All this was said very rapidly . . .

. . . 'I will readily grant you, Sir, that the *patriots* as they are

75 pleased to call themselves in Holland have been extremely desirous to make proselytes to their doctrines everywhere. But it is not from them alone that my subjects in the Netherlands have borrowed the spirit of turbulent and mistaken patriotism. It is a flaming forth in every petty state of that quarter of Europe. Not only at Liège,
80 at Spa, and at Aix-la-Chapelle, but even in the Princess Cunegunda of Saxony's abbey of Essen! Nay, let me tell you,' continued the Emperor, 'but only in the way of confidential conversation, that the King of France has acted very *unwisely*, not to use a *harsher* term, to have the seeds of that fructifying doctrine in his own
85 dominions by his late *assembly of the Notables* – he may expect the inevitable growth of them throughout the whole of his future reign. . . .'

Memoirs and Correspondence of Sir Robert Murray Keith, K.B. (2 vols, 1849), II, pp 208–18

Questions

   a Why did Maria Theresa say in 1775 that only 26 of the last 36 years had been happy for her (lines 6–14)?
   b 'Absolutist rather than liberal.' Do you agree with this criticism of Joseph's Instructions to his District Commissioners?
   c What was the Assembly of Notables (line 85)?
★ *d* Why was opposition to Joseph II's reforms especially strong in the Netherlands and Hungary?

V The Century's Wars

Introduction

Evan Luard in *War in International Society* (1986) has emphasised the importance in eighteenth-century hostilities of 'the military technology of the age: the low level of mobility, the importance attached to fortification and siege warfare, the cautious and economical methods of campaigning', because this largely determined 'the form of warfare that was now generally practised, involving long sieges, elaborate manoeuvres and often the deliberate avoidance of large-scale battles'. Because there was normally little fighting in the winter, wars were lengthy, but they were not intensive and were generally fought by professional armies of limited size for restricted objectives.

Frederick the Great inevitably was influenced by the circumstances of the times during the Seven Years War. Prussia was virtually surrounded by enemies. He had to defend his territory and not dissipate his outnumbered troops. He sought to take advantage of his two valuable assets – a better-trained and disciplined army and his central position. He tried always to maintain the initiative, to attack first one enemy and then another, to gather at a decisive point a superior force and gain what triumph he could there. He wrote in 1759, 'I have so many enemies that I have no choice but to attack. . . . I have only kept going by attacking whenever I can and by scoring little advantages which add up.' Only when he was unable to take the initiative in such favourable circumstances did he regretfully resort to what he called 'the emetic of a battle'. He knew that such a full-size confrontation might mean the destruction of his valuable army as at Kunersdorf, described in the extract from the letter (p 54 below) written by him to his Foreign Minister after the battle he fought against the Austrians and Russians, in which he only escaped disaster because his enemies did not follow up their victory.

The general circumstances of warfare at that time led Clausewitz to allege that the armies became 'a State within a State in which the elements of violence gradually faded away'. And he was certain about the cause of the changes that took place in warfare during the later part of the eighteenth century. The wars of the earlier years had been fought by kings with calculated intensity and for limited objectives; but in 1793 war became the concern of the people and its scope boundless.

This interpretation of the situation has, however, been a matter of dispute. Military historians have sometimes challenged it and questioned the military importance of the French Revolution. They have rather regarded the changes as the culmination of a series of developments in the conditions of war which took place over a period before 1789, which meant that the weapons used in the Revolutionary and Napoleonic Wars had been designed during those years and the military commanders trained under the old regime.

This was certainly true of the French army. Defeat in the Seven Years War stimulated it to adopt important innovations, particularly in the introduction of light artillery, which could be massed at a decisive point and used with infantry. This enabled armies to be divided into smaller units, and at the same time military writers expressed the need for flexibility, speed and aggression in fighting.

Nevertheless, the old regime still lacked two conditions necessary for the realisation of these ideas – a suitable kind of army and a commander capable of carrying them out. The French revolutionary forces supplied the first and Napoleon the second. The government of the new French Republic found itself threatened along its frontiers by three great powers and yet was ready to wage a war of liberation throughout the continent, but possessed only an army which had virtually integrated. By means of the *levée en masse* it gained thousands of fresh recruits, while revolutionary fervour gave it a new determination and driving force. Circumstances meant that it operated, in the words of Lefebvre, through 'continual improvisation', it lived off the country and sacrificed everything to mobility and a quick, decisive attack.

This army was used with outstanding success by Napoleon as the Duke of Wellington recognised (p 58 below). He instilled in his Grand Army a pride and self-confidence which helped it to gain its victories. It was solely under his command, and he used it to win a contest in a single, annihilating campaign. His ways of war, particularly his use of artillery, brought heavy casualties. Eventually France could no longer stand such losses, and his enemies could resist and defeat him.

1 The War of the Austrian Succession (1740–8)

(a) Frederick's invasion of Silesia

Silesia is the portion of the Imperial heritage to which we have the strongest claim and which is the most suitable for the House of Brandenburg. It is consonant with justice to maintain one's rights and to seize the opportunity of the Emperor's death to take possession. The superiority of our troops, the promptitude with which we can set them in motion, in a word the clear advantage we have over our neighbours, gives us in this unexpected emergency an infinite superiority over all other powers in Europe. If we wait until Saxony and Bavaria start hostilities, we could not prevent the aggrandisement of the former which is wholly contrary to our interests. If we act at once we keep her in subjection and by cutting off the supply of horses prevent her from moving. England and France are foes. If France meddles in the affairs of the Empire, England could not allow it, so I can always make a good alliance with one or the other. England could not be jealous of my getting Silesia, which would do her no harm, and she needs allies. Holland will not care, all the more since the loans of the Amsterdam business world secured on Silesia will be guaranteed. If we cannot arrange with England and Holland, we can certainly make a deal with France, who cannot frustrate our designs and will welcome the abasement of the Imperial house. Russia alone might cause trouble. . . . All this leads to the conclusion that we must occupy Silesia before the winter and then negotiate. When we are in possession we can negotiate with success. We should never get anything by mere negotiations except very onerous conditions in return for a few trifles.

Frederick II, *Memorandum of 1740*, in G. P. Gooch, *Frederick the Great* (1947), pp 6–7

(b) The election of the Emperor Charles VII, 1742

. . . The proclamation was read in German. In substance it declared that, as the Imperial throne had become vacant as a result of the death of Charles VI, the Electoral College, acting in conformity with the laws, had chosen the Elector of Bavaria as King of the Romans, with one voice . . . and that everyone had to recognise him as such. Then the herald cried out 'Vivat rex' and those who were in the choir (almost all of them Frenchmen) showed this by echoing the cry, and immediately afterwards the cannon on the rampart was fired. It should be noted here that there was not the least sign of exultation in the town. On the contrary everybody had a serious air, and almost all Germany was very grieved by this election. The reason was that the election was felt to be entirely a French achievement; it was even regarded as having been made to a certain extent under compulsion from the two French armies in Bohemia and Westphalia. It was said that this Emperor had been chosen to suit the French, and that he was the creature of the Cardinal [Fleury] and the brothers Belle-Isle. It was felt that this Emperor, even if he obtained Bohemia and Upper Austria, could not put eighteen thousand men in the field and so could not hold his own against France, to which country he really owed the Empire. For this reason France had become dominant in the Empire, especially as she had divided the princes into parties of equal strength. Above all the Elector of Bavaria and the princes of his house had made themselves hated because, having been obliged to undertake greater expenses than they could bear, they had bled their country, and Bavaria was in a pitiable condition. So this day was marvellous for France and for the Cardinal and the brothers Belle-Isle, since the Empire recognised that they had given it an Emperor. For this purpose each of the interested princes had been given the share that was most appropriate to him in the spoils of the House of Austria; which house was annihilated as a result. All this was more than the Empire could stomach, accustomed as it had been for so long to recognise that family as its master.

Mémoires de Prince de Croy-Solre. Revue d'histoire diplomatique (1894), p 595, in H. Butterfield, op cit, pp 10–11

(c) The Treaty of Aix-la-Chapelle, 1748

II Mutual restitution shall be made of conquests acquired since the beginning of the present war, both in Europe and in the East and West Indies, in the state in which they stand at present.

III Dunkirk shall remain fortified on the land side, in the state in which it stands at present, but on the side of the sea it shall remain on the footing of the former treaties.

IV The Duchies of Parma, Piacenza and Guastalla shall be ceded to the Most Serene Infante Don Philip and shall serve as an establishment for him, with right of reversion to its present possessor, after H.M. the King of the Two Sicilies has crossed over to take the Crown of Spain, as also in the event of the Most Serene Infante Don Philip dying without heirs.

VII H.M. the King of Sardinia shall remain in possession of everything he has held either by old right or recent acquisition, and particularly the lands he acquired in 1743, the Vigevanasco, part of the Pavesan, and the County of Anghiera, in the state that he possesses them to-day, in virtue of the cessions which were made to him then.

X The Assiento Treaty, concerning the traffic in Negroes, signed in Madrid, 26 March 1713, and the article concerning the annual ship, are specially confirmed by the present Preliminary Articles, for the years of their non-operation (i.e. for four years).

XIV The Prince elected to the Imperial dignity shall be recognised in this quality by all the Powers which have not yet recognised him.

XIX All the Powers interested in the present Preliminary Articles shall renew in the best possible form the guarantee of the Pragmatic

Sanction of 19th April 1713 . . . with the exception, however, of the cessions already made by the said Princess [Maria Theresa] and those stipulated in the present Preliminary Articles.

90 XX The Duchy of Silesia and the County of Glatz, as they are now possessed by His Prussian Majesty, shall be guaranteed to this Prince by all the Powers and Contracting Parties who have signed the present Preliminary Articles.

F. W. W. Wenck, op cit, II, pp 310–16, in H. Butterfield, op cit, pp 12–13

Questions

a 'Take first and argue afterwards'. How did Frederick justify his seizure of Silesia?
b 'Almost all Germany was grieved' (line 37) and 'this day was marvellous for France' (line 53). Why was there this different attitude towards the election of Charles Albert as Emperor?
c What were 'the Electoral College' (line 29) and 'the Assiento Treaty' (line 78)? Who were 'the brothers Belle-Isle' (line 43) and 'the Most Serene Infante Don Philip' (line 67)?
★ d Why did the saying '*Bête comme la Paix*' express French disappointment with the Treaty of Aix-la-Chapelle?

2 The Seven Years War (1756–63)

(a) Frederick's Memorandum to the British Government, 1756

They thought in France that orders from Versailles would be blindly followed, and Prussia was blamed for not carrying fire and sword into the Electorate of Hanover. The late Franco-Prussian Treaty was never an offensive alliance, and the neutrality convention
5 to which France so strongly objects was an instrument for preserving Europe from a war in which only French and English were concerned for their colonial possessions. In their first fury the Versailles Ministers resented my pretended disobedience to their orders; then they softened their tone, but they had already gone
10 too far. The Court of Vienna knew something of my negotiations and was angry to see its hopes disappointed. It had counted on Prussia attacking Hanover and on utilising the opportunity with the aid of Russia to recover Silesia. It regards the King of Prussia as an obstacle to its vast designs, believing that if it can be eliminated
15 the rest will be easy. Accepting the highest bid, Russia will doubtless follow the counsels of the Court of Vienna, and France will doubtless pay Russia the subsidies hitherto received from England. Such is the present European situation. The equilibrium is destroyed, both as regards the Great Powers and within the Empire.
20 The evil is great but not without remedy. . . . Germany is threatened with great calamities. Prussia is faced with war, but all

these difficulties do not dismay her. Three things can restore the balance of Europe: the intimate union of two courts, new alliances and courage.

G. P. Gooch, *Frederick the Great*, pp 34–5

(b) Frederick's self-justification, 1756

25 It is true that the King begins hostilities; but since this term is often confused with aggression, and since the Court of Vienna is always seeking to incriminate Prussia, the meaning must be explained. By aggression one understands any opposed to the meaning of a treaty of peace. A League for offensive purposes, incitement to war
30 against a third power, the plan of invading the territories of another prince, a sudden invasion: all these are aggressions. Whoever anticipates them may commit hostilities, but he is not the aggressor. . . . Since the Court of Vienna resolves to infringe treaties guaranteed by all the powers of Europe; since its ambition bursts
35 the most sacred barriers against human cupidity; since it aims at tyrannising over the German Empire; since its vast designs involve the overthrow of this republic of princes which it is the duty of Emperors to maintain, the King has decided to oppose the enemies of his country and to frustrate this odious project. His Majesty
40 declares that the liberties of the Germanic Body will only be buried in the same grave as Prussia. He calls heaven to witness that, having vainly tried to preserve his own country and all Germany from the scourge of war, he is forced to take up arms in order to destroy a conspiracy against his possessions and his crown. He only abandons
45 his habitual moderation because it ceases to be a virtue when it is a question of defending his honour, his independence, his country and his crown.

'Exposé des Motifs qui ont obligé sa Majesté le Roi de Prusse à prevenir les dessins de la Cour de Vienne', *Preussische Staatsschriften aus der Regierungszeity Friedrichs des Grossen*, eds R. Koser and F. Krauske (3 vols, 1876), III, p 181, in G. P. Gooch, op cit, p 39

(c) Frederick's defeat at Kunersdorf, 1759

I attacked the enemy at 11 o'clock this morning. We pushed them to the cemetery of the Jews near Frankfort [on the Oder]; all my
50 troops did marvels, but this cemetery cost us a prodigious number of men. Our troops were put to confusion; I rallied them three times; at the finish I thought I should be taken myself, and I was forced to give up the field. My uniform is riddled with shots; I had

two horses killed: my misfortune is still to be alive; our loss is very considerable. Of an army of 48 000 men I have not 3 000 at the present moment; all are in flight, and I have lost control. You will do well to look after your safety in Berlin. It is a cruel reverse; I shall not survive it; the consequences of this business will be worse than the defeat itself. I have no more resources, and to tell you the truth I think all is lost. I shall not go on living after the loss of my country. Goodbye for ever.

Lord Mahon, *History of England from the Peace of Utrecht to the Peace of Versailles* (7 vols, 1858), IV, p xxxi

(d) Choiseul's Memorandum, 1765

I then proposed to Your Majesty two games to play together: one to keep up the negotiation in England in such a way that if it did not succeed this time it would serve from its simplicity as a base from the general negotiation which must take place if Pitt fell before the influence of Bute. At the same time – and this was the second game which I thought essential – I entered into an exchange of views with Spain, so devised that if we were to make peace that Crown would find it to its interests in the negotiation, and guarantee the stability of the treaty. If, on the contrary, we failed in this, my plan was that Spain should be drawn into the war, and that France would be able to profit by events which this new complication might produce, and repair her losses. Finally if the event proved unfortunate, I had in view that the losses of Spain would lighten those which France might suffer.

J. S. Corbett, *England in the Seven Years War* (2 vols, 1907), II, p 185

(e) The Treaties of Paris and Hubertsburg, 1763

So on February 10th 1763 the French and British concluded the Peace of Paris whereby the British secured Canada, Nova Scotia and the rights of navigation on the Mississippi throughout the Middle West down to the Gulf, and also acquired the important base of Minorca, as well as Florida, from Spain. They also retained Gibraltar and secured more West Indian islands, but Havana and Manila in the Philippines, both captured by the British Navy, and strategically important bases against the oceanic trade of the Spanish Colonial Empire, were restored to Spain. On the other hand, British paramountcy in India was *de facto* recognized. Thus the French, though stripped of vast potentially rich areas of Empire both in North America and the East, were not, as Pitt had intended, crippled at sea. Great Britain retained enormous gains, but not all that Pitt had hoped for.

90 Frederick II, who signed the Peace of Hubertsburg with Austria, in the same month and year, gave up Saxony, but retained Silesia with its textile and metallurgical wealth, both vital to the Prussian economy, reoccupied East Prussia and remained poised, a first rate military power, to take his share of a probable partition of a
95 disintegrating Poland.

John Bowle, *A History of Europe 1979*, p 470

Questions

a Do extracts *a*, *b* and *c* explain why Frederick followed a hostile policy, but tried to avoid battle whenever possible?
b How did Choiseul put into effect his policy outlined in extract *d*?
c What is there to suggest in extract *c* that the peace settlement of 1763 was likely to create dangerous ambitions and dissatisfactions among the powers in the future?
* *d* 'The Seven Years War was the logical outcome of the rivalries engendered in the course of the War of the Austrian Succession'. Do you agree?

3   The Revolutionary War (1792–1802)

(a) The nature of the war

In 1793 a force appeared that beggared all imagination. Suddenly war again became the business of the people – a people of thirty millions, all of whom considered themselves to be citizens. . . . The people became a participant in war; instead of government
5 and armies as heretofore, the full weight of the nation was thrown into the balance. The resources and efforts now available for use surpassed all conventional limit; nothing now impeded the vigour with which war could now be waged. . . .

Various factors powerfully increased that vigour: the vastness of
10 available resources, the ample field of opportunity, and the depth of feeling generally aroused. The sole aim of war was generally to overthrow the opponent. Not until he was prostrate was it considered possible to pause and try to reconcile the opposing interests.
15 War, untrammelled by any conventional restraints, had broken loose in all its elemental fury. This was due to the people's new share in the great affairs of state; and their participation, in turn, resulted partly from the impact that the revolution had on the internal conditions of every state and partly from the danger that
20 France posed to everyone.

Carl von Clausewitz, *On War*, ed. and trans., Michael Howard and Peter Paret (1976), Book 8, Chapter 3

(b) Danton's speech, 1792

It is satisfying for the ministers of a free people to have announced to them that their fatherland will be saved. Everyone is stirred, everyone is roused, everyone longs for the fight. You know that Verdun is not yet in the power of our enemies. You know that the garrison has promised to put to death the first man who wishes to surrender. A part of the people will go to the frontiers, another will dig trenches, and a third, armed with spikes, will defend the centres of the towns. Paris will support these great efforts. The commissioners of the Commune will proclaim, in a solemn manner, the invitation to the citizens to arm themselves and march for the defence of the fatherland. It is at this moment, gentlemen, that you can declare that the capital has deserved well of the whole of France. It is at this moment that the National Assembly will demand a true committee of war. We demand that you co-operate with us in guiding the highest efforts of the people, by naming the commissioners who will assist in these great undertakings. We demand that anyone who refuses to serve in person, or to offer his arms, should be punished by death.

We demand that this should be made an instruction to the citizens to guide their efforts. We demand that it should be sent by messengers in all the departments to inform them of the decrees which you will issue.

The alarm which will be sounded is not a signal of fear; it is the attack on the enemies of the fatherland. (Applause) To defeat them we must have audacity, more audacity, always audacity, and France is saved. (Renewed applause)

> Speech to the National Assembly, 2 September 1792, in H. Morse-Stephens, *Orators of the French Revolution* (2 vols, 1892), II, p 170

(c) The Edict of Fraternity, 1792

The National Convention declares in the name of the French nation that it will accord fraternity and assistance to all peoples who wish to recover their liberty. It charges the executive power to give the generals the necessary orders for bearing help to these peoples and defending citizens who are vexed for the cause of liberty. The present decree shall be translated and printed in all languages.

> H. Butterfield, *Select Documents*, pp 74–5

(d) Napoleonic warfare (1)

The [French] army of 1792–5 really was 'the people's army' by all criteria applicable in such matters, worked up to combat zeal not so much by the soldier's usual closest allegiances (regiment, officers, general, national leader) but by conscious devotion to the *patrie* and the Revolution. Napoleon's army, evolved from this, retained many of its characteristics while adopting a different ethos. It was still popular enough. Its victories, its achievements, its sufferings and as time went by its defeats evoked appropriate responses of admiration and condolence (with some help in the orchestration by the Emperor and his opinion-managers). It was still democratic, so far as effective armies can internally be. Many ways continued to be open from the bottom to the top, discipline remained relatively free and easy, officers and men did not live worlds apart (egalitarian aspects of army life which '*le petit caporal*' sedulously cultivated). . . .

But in some essential respects it was increasingly a State within a State, less responsibly rooted in French society than it used to be. . . . [It] became more and more professional and self-sufficient. . . . He had the supreme leader's talent of inspiring devotion among his followers and of making others imagine that they would have liked to follow too. Above all a soldier himself, he was above all a soldier's man. But it was not only to soldiers that he successfully appealed. The French people evidently did not now much wish to be soldiers themselves, but Napoleon's army, so long as it fought in other countries and there gained glory and victories remained highly interesting to them. Meantime, whatever tendencies towards popular militarism were already there from before the years of his despotism (and obviously there were plenty), he only strengthened and consolidated. Everything he did to French government and society was cut after the military pattern. There is no evidence that the French people found it uncongenial.

Geoffrey Best, *War and Society in Revolutionary Europe, 1770–1870* (1982), pp 111–12

(e) Napoleonic warfare (2)

[Napoleon] was the sovereign of the country as well as the military chief of the army. That country was constituted upon a military basis. All its institutions were framed for the purpose of forming and maintaining its army with a view to conquest. All the offices and rewards of the State were reserved in the first instance exclusively for the army. An officer, even a private soldier, might look to the sovereignty of a kingdom as a reward for his service.

Philip Henry, Fifth Earl Stanhope, *Notes of Conversations with the Duke of Wellington 1831–1851* (1888), p 81

(f) Napoleon's Proclamation to his Army in Egypt

Headquarters on board the *Orient*, 22nd June 1798

Soldiers, You are going to carry out a conquest the effects of which upon the civilisation and commerce of the world are beyond all calculation.

You will give England the most definite and palpable blow that could be given, pending the day when you are able to give her the death-blow.

We shall make some tiring marches; we shall be engaged in several battles; but we shall succeed in all that we undertake, for destiny is on our side.

The Mameluke Beys who give all their favour to English commerce, and have overwhelmed our merchants with humiliations, and who tyrannise over the unfortunate inhabitants of the Nile region, will have ended their existence within a few days after our arrival.

The people amongst who you are going to live will be Mohammedans; the first article of their faith is that 'There is no other God save God and Mohammed is his prophet'.

Do not contradict them; treat them as we treated the Jews and the Italians; pay due respect to their muftis and imams, as you did to the rabbis and bishops.

Show the same toleration to the mosques and to the ceremonies prescribed in the Koran, and you showed to the convents and synagogues, to the religions of Moses and Jesus Christ.

The Roman legions gave protection to all religions. You will find that the customs here are different from those of Europe; however, you must get used to them.

The people amongst whom we are going to live do not treat women as we treat them; but in all countries he who violates is a monster.

Plundering only enriches a small number of men; it dishonours us, and destroys our resources, and it makes us enemies of the people whom it is our interest to have as our friends.

The first town you will come to was built by Alexander. We shall find memories worthy of the imitation of Frenchmen at every step of the way.

Correspondance de Napoleon Ier (32 vols, 1858–69), IV, No. 2710, in H. Butterfield, op cit, pp 77–8

Questions

a What changes do the above extracts show the French Revolution made in military organisation and how did politicians and commanders respond to them?

b What were 'the Commune' (line 29), 'the National Assembly' (line 33), 'the National Convention' (line 47) and 'the Mameluke Beys' (line 101)?

c   What was the 'most definite and palpable blow' (line 95) which Napoleon hoped to inflict upon Britain through his Egyptian campaign?

★ d   How was Napoleon able to obtain conditions favourable to France in the Treaty of Amiens (1802)?

4   The Napoleonic War (1803–15)

(a) An incident in the Austrian campaign, 1805

Twenty-Fifth Bulletin of the Grand Army, Schoenbrun, November 26 – In the late war, the 76th regiment of the line lost two standards in the Grison, which circumstance was, for a long time, the subject of deep affliction to the whole corps. These brave fellows, conscious
5 that Europe had not forgotten their disgrace, though their courage was uncensurable, were so fortunate as to find the subjects of their lost honour in the arsenal at Inspruck [after its capture]. Happily they were recognised by an officer. All the soldiers crowded around him; and Marshal Ney, being informed of the particulars, ordered
10 the colours to be restored to the 76th with great ceremony. Tears fell from the eyes of all the veterans; and the conscripts felt themselves elated in the assistance they had given in the recovery of the honours snatched from their comrades by the chances of war. The Emperor has ordered that the remembrance of the
15 affecting scene should be consecrated by a tablet. The French soldier maintains a sentiment for his colours, bordering upon tenderness; they are the object of his affections, equally with a present from his mistress.

The Times, 10 December 1805

(b) Napoleon to his Army after victory, 1805

Headquarters at Austerlitz, December 3, 1805
20 Soldiers, I am satisfied with you. In the battle of Austerlitz you have justified what I expected from your intrepidity. You have covered yourselves with eternal glory. An army of one hundred thousand men, which was commanded by the Emperors of Russia and Austria, has been in less than four hours cut off or dispersed.
25 Those that escaped your swords have thrown themselves into the lakes. Forty stands of colours, the stands of the Russian imperial guard, one hundred and twenty pieces of cannon, twenty generals

and above thirty thousand prisoners are the fruits of this ever-memorable battle. Their infantry, so celebrated and so superior to you in numbers, has proved unable to resist your charge, and henceforth you have no rivals to fear.

Thus in less than two months the third coalition is conquered and dissolved. Peace cannot be far off; but, as I promised my people before crossing the Rhine, I will conclude it only upon terms consistent with my pledge, which shall secure not only the indemnification, but the reward, of my allies.

Soldiers, when the French people placed the imperial crown upon my head I trusted to you to enable me to maintain it in that splendour of glory which alone could give it value in my estimation. But at that moment my enemies entertained the design of tarnishing and degrading it; and the iron crown, which was gained by the blood of so many Frenchmen, they would have compelled me to place on the head of my bitterest foe, – an extravagant and foolish proposal, which you have brought to naught on the anniversary of your emperor's coronation. You have taught them that it is easier to defy and threaten than to subdue us.

Soldiers, when everything necessary to the security, the happiness, and the prosperity of our country has been achieved, I will return you my thanks in France. Then will you be the objects of my tenderest care. My people will receive you with rapture and joy. To say to me, 'I was in the battle of Austerlitz', will be enough to authorise the reply, 'That is a brave man.'

Napoleon

Annual Register (1805), pp 665f.

(c) Wellington to his younger brother, Henry Wellesley

Celorico [in Spain], 11 June 1810

This *bicoque* has been in part invested for nearly two months; and a fortnight has elapsed since the guns moved from Salamanca; and the French are not yet in possession of the ground they must have for the siege. This is not the way in which they have conquered Europe! Having obliged the French to collect an army for this enterprise, that is, to make the attack of the worst fortified place in the world, I fear I can do no more for it. I think that I might have delayed still longer the complete investment of the place, and the chances of war and chapter of accidents, which in these days are not allowed to be counted for anything, might have enabled me to prevent the siege altogether, if the government possessed any strength, or desired to have anything done but what is *safe and cheap*. But, with an army considerably inferior in numbers, consisting of a large proportion of troops of a doubtful description, which are scarcely formed, and the enemy being infinitely (three times) superior in cavalry, I think I ought not now to risk a general action to relieve the place.

However, I do not yet give the matter up. The defence of a Spanish place must not be reckoned upon according to the ordinary rules. If they will defend themselves as others have, the French must feel the consequences of Massena having weakened every other point to collect this large army; and if he should be induced to reduce it at all, I shall be at hand to assist and relieve them.

I have no doubt whatever but that the French feel, throughout the Peninsula, the inadequacy even of the large force they have in it, to complete the conquest and to establish and support the government; and the continued hostility of the people must distress them much. All the intercepted correspondence tends to show their misery and despondence. Although they may succeed in taking Ciudad Rodrigo, it does not follow that even the force which they have collected will be sufficient to oblige us to evacuate the Peninsula; and as long as we shall not shrink, the cause will not be lost. . . .

H. Wragg (ed.), *Letters Written in War-Time* (1915)

(d) Napoleon's downfall

If he did not win his battle, Napoleon's entire strategy was ruined. Although he did not ignore problems of supply, and indeed made careful preparations at the outset of every campaign, the speed with which he drove on his armies made it impossible for their supply columns to keep up. They thus had to a large extent to live off the country as had their predecessors in the Thirty Years War [1618–48]. Napoleon expected his troops to fend for themselves, which indeed they did, though they did not make the French cause very popular in the process. But when the size of armies ran into six figures, they could only do this for short periods, and so long as they kept on the move. For more prolonged subsistence they relied on capturing the enemy's magazines after the battle and then forcing the defeated country to support them. But when in 1807 Napoleon began to penetrate into the less fertile areas of Europe, into Poland after the battle of Eylau, and into the Iberian peninsula, supply became a nagging and insoluble problem. The secret of Wellington's success in the Peninsula lay in the cool ruthlessness with which he exploited and exacerbated the French supply difficulties while ensuring that he should have none of his own. The success of the Russians in 1812 rested on their ability to deny Napoleon his decisive battle and permit him to advance into their country to a far deeper extent than his supply arrangements could cover. Winter and starvation did the rest. In the three years left to him Napoleon had to confine himself to operations of more traditional scope; and

110 the traditional talents conserved by the armies of his opponents were able to show up to a better effect.

Michael Howard, *War in European History* (1967), pp 85–6

Questions

a What do extracts *a* and *b* reveal about the relationship between Napoleon and his soldiers?
b Explain Napoleon's reference to his enemies in lines 40–6.
c How do extracts *b* and *c* suggest that Wellington used his limited manpower to wear down the French in Spain?
★ d What were the main military and political causes of Napoleon's final failure?

VI The French Monarchy

Introduction

The history of the French monarchy during the eighteenth century inevitably presents those who study it with considerable difficulties. The regime was destroyed before the end of the century as the result of a revolution which, however great a shock it was to contemporaries, can only be understood by an investigation of the past. This has meant that there has been a tendency to regard this period of French history in the light of its conclusion, to consider it important because of its result. The German historian, Leopold von Ranke, has said, however, that 'every age is equal in the sight of God', and this period must be recognised as complete in itself with its own character and problems and participants, who were engaged solely with the contemporary situation as they saw it.

Upon the death of Louis XIV in 1715, important classes in the kingdom were looking to the past rather than to the future. There was an aristocratic reaction which wanted to return to an imaginary time before the Cardinals Richelieu and Mazarin had destroyed the liberties of the nobility. Their hopes rested upon the Duke of Orleans, who now became Regent since the new King – Louis XV – was only five years old. He attempted to institute constitutional reforms that would bring this hope about. The Parlement of Paris was informed of the replacement of the Secretaries of State by the *Polysynodie*, which gave the nobles representation in the government, and the restoration of the Parlement's right of Remonstrance, allowing it to refuse to register royal edicts. Both these experiments failed. In 1718 the *Polysynodie* was abolished, and the Parlement was reminded of the Crown's prerogatives at a *Lit de Justice*. Another duke, Saint-Simon, who had supported these reforms, said that their failure was due to the ignorance, levity and inconstancy of the nobility, who were capable only of being killed in war.

Three years after the death of Orleans in 1723, Cardinal Fleury gained control of the government. He wished to follow a pacific foreign policy so that France in future took no part in great wars, which would give the country an opportunity to recover from the disasters of Louis XIV's reign and achieve positive economic advances. In his letter (p 66 below) to the Spanish court, he outlined his reasons for keeping France at peace, but this was written towards the end of his career when the Austrian succession question was threatening war, and his policy was being threatened by the war party in France. He was reluctantly to be drawn into war that year. Nevertheless, his policy did restore economic prosperity to France, which became a wealthy country, but one where there was poverty also – mainly among the rural population.

Louis XV began his personal rule in 1743. The extracts (pp 67–8 below) from the journals of two politicians in 1747 both assert the chaotic relationship that prevailed between the King and his ministers, but the comments of the Marquis D'Argenson need to be considered with caution. He wrote with bitterness because he had been dismissed from the post of Foreign Minister less than a month previously following French reverses in the war. The Comte de Maurepas, upon whom he commented, was, in fact, a capable and successful Minister of Marine under whom the French navy was strengthened.

The Parlement of Paris took to adopting the policy of combining with the provincial parlements in opposition to the governments. In 1770 the King condemned its behaviour in an edict (p 69 below), which was followed the next year by the banishment of its members to the provinces. He still on this occasion claimed to rule by divine right and to possess supreme power, but his authority was, in fact, limited by political checks, local rights and relics of feudalism.

After the accession of Louis XVI in 1774, the crisis of the *ancien régime* deepened. The government was now being undermined by the growing financial difficulties of the Crown. The cost of the wars fought by France during the eighteenth century, culminating in the American War of Independence, had been beyond the resources of the royal treasury. Attempts at reform failed through differences over the nature of the constitutional changes to be made. Means of increasing the national revenue had to overcome the opposition of the privileged classes, who would be affected by taxation. The calling of the Assembly of Notables in 1787 tried to achieve this. Its failure may be regarded as making it inevitable that reform would be replaced by revolution.

1 The Regency and Fleury

(a) *The Polysynodie, 1715*

Besides the Council of Regency, to which all business will be referred, it is necessary to establish a Council of War, a Council of Finance, a Council of Foreign Affairs and a Council for the Internal Affairs of the Kingdom; it is judged equally important to form a
5 Council of Conscience . . . and it is hoped that the Parlement will

allow it to include some of their magistrates who, by their ability and knowledge, could there uphold the rights and liberties of the Gallican Church.

J. Flammeront, *Remonstrances du Parlement de Paris au XVIIIe siècle* (2 vols, 1889), I, p 20

(b) The Right of Remonstrance, 1715

Our court of Parlement has permission to make what representation it considers fit to us, before being obliged to the registration of the edicts and declarations which we shall forward to it, and we are persuaded that it will exercise the ancient liberty which we restore to it with such wisdom and care, that its advice will contribute only to the good of our state and will always deserve to be confirmed by our authority.

Ibid., I, p vi

(c) The Lit de Justice, 1718

Laws, new and old, only exist by the will of the sovereign and are made legal only by this will; their registration in the courts, which have been entrusted with this task, adds nothing to the power of the legislator; it is merely the promulgation of laws, and an indispensable act of obedience which the courts should observe and no doubt will observe as a point of honour in giving an example to other subjects of the king.

Ibid., I, p 86

(d) Fleury's peace-policy, 1740

Cardinal Fleury to Philip V and Elizabeth Farnese of Spain, 24th November 1740 – We have our hands tied on the subject of the Pragmatic Sanction, and even if we had not already been bound by the Treaty of Vienna [1738], I do not know whether we should not have been compelled to accept this arrangement to avoid a general war, which would have been as dangerous for Spain as for us.

Your Majesties are aware of the expenses which we have to meet both to keep up our existing squadrons and to prepare the further ones we shall need in the coming year; especially as provisions and all the munitions necessary for these armaments are so excessively dear.

But what concerns us still more is the frightful distress in the provinces caused by the dearth of corn and all the grains necessary for subsistence. The principal duty of a King is the relief of all his subjects, and, apart from the immense relief which we are obliged to grant, Your Majesties will easily understand what a great decrease there has been in the amount of taxes which we are able to collect, as the result of the poverty of the people. . . .

> Maurice Sautai, *Les Préliminaires de la guerre de la succession d'Autriche* (1907), p 488, in H. Butterfield, *Select Documents*, pp 7–8

Questions

a   What were the *Polysynodie* and the *Lit de Justice*?
b   How did the Parlement of Paris and the Crown differ over the nature of the Right of Remonstrance (extracts *b* and *c*)?
c   How was French policy affected by the Pragmatic Sanction and the Treaty of Vienna (lines 25–6)?
* d   Account for the failure of the constitutional reforms attempted by the Duke of Orleans.

2   Weakness and Contention

(a) Louis XV and his ministers in 1747 (1)

It seems that, though he does much himself, his ministers easily exert a strong influence on his decision, for he refers almost everything to them. And so, since he has no principal minister, each as such in his own department, where he can do almost as he wishes, although with caution and fear of reports by their enemies to the king who tries to do well and wishes to be instructed. He does, indeed, take some care over this, but perhaps not enough, or he does not do it well himself.

> Duc de Croy, *Journal inédit*, eds Vicomte de Grouchy and P. Cottin (4 vols, 1906–7), I, p 92

(b) Louis XV and his ministers in 1747 (2)

M de Maurepas increases in favour with the king, while I have been dismissed from my ministry because, showing with sincerity the necessity of peace (however made), I brought forward the means of doing so, while others retrograded. I formed for the king a strong party in Germany, both for the present moment and for that succeeding the peace; I smoothed his enemies; I preserved and inspired his friends; above all, I showed by my conduct that confidence could be placed in our sincerity.

M de Maurepas is inexcusable in allowing our navy to run down;

the parsimony of the late cardinal is no valid excuse; a zealous and intelligent man manages to do the little he has to do the best he can. Has he yet ever made a journey to any of the ports? He prefers an idle, intriguing life in Paris to all that urgent duty suggests for so essential a minister.

They tell an amusing tale in public of how the king dreamed the other night about cats; he saw four of them fighting; one thin, one fat, one blind of an eye, one blind in both eyes. A faithful valet explained to him his dream thus: 'The thin cat is your people; the fat cat is the financiers; the one-eyed cat is your council; and the blind cat is your Majesty, who does not choose to see anything.'

  Katherine Prescott Wormeley (ed.), *Journal and Memories of the Marquis d'Argenson* (2 vols, 1905), pp 2–3

(c) The threat of revolution

25 December 1753 – Wherever you are, inform yourself minutely of, and attend particularly to, the affairs of France; they grow serious, and, in my opinion, will grow more and more so every day. The King is despised, and I do not wonder at it, but he has brought it about to be hated at the same time, which seldom happens to the same man. His Ministers are known to be as disunited as incapable; he hesitates between the Church and the Parliaments, like the ass in the fable, that starved between two hampers of hay; too much in love with his mistress to part with her; jealous of the Parliaments which would support his authority; and a devoted bigot to the Church that would destroy it.

The people are poor, consequently discontented; those who have religion are divided in their notions of it; which is saying that they hate one another. The Clergy never do forgive; much less will they forgive the Parliament; the Parliament will never forgive them. The Army must, without doubt, take, in their minds at least, different parts in all these disputes, which, upon occasion, would break out. . . . The French nation reasons freely, which they never did before, upon matters of religion and government, and begin to be *spregiudicati*; the officers do so too; in short, all the symptoms which I have ever met with in history, previous to great changes and revolutions in Government now exist, and daily increase in France. I am glad of it; the rest of Europe will be the quieter, and have time to recover.

  Lord Chesterfield, *Letters to his Son* (Everyman edition, 1929), pp 275–6

(d) The King and the Parlement

Edict of the King, December 1770 – The spirit of system, which is as uncertain in its principles as it is bold in its enterprises, has not only made disastrous inroads upon the realm of religion and morals; it has refused even to respect the deliberations of several of our courts. We have seen these courts in their turn put forward new ideas and hazard principles which they would have proscribed as being calculated to disturb public order, if they had found them at any other time or in any other body than themselves.

We have seen them at various times resort to interruptions and cessations of service, thereby making our subjects suffer from delays in the administration of justice . . . and they have imagined that by such methods they could constrain us to give way to their opposition.

At other times they have sent in their combined resignation, and by a singular piece of contradiction they have disputed our right to accept the resignations a moment later.

Finally they have come to consider themselves as forming one single body, one single parlement ranged into different grades over the different parts of our kingdom.

This novelty was first conceived of by our Parlement of Paris, which then ignored it when it served its purpose to ignore it. But it still exists in our other parlements; it is reproduced in their decrees and decisions . . . as though our courts could forget that several of them existed in provinces that did not belong to our kingdom at all, but have come into our possession by private titles; also that they were established separately at different dates; that our predecessors made them independent of one another at their formation and gave them no claim to relationship with one another; that their founders gave them limits which we or our successors may extend or reduce as the interests of our people demand it; and finally that beyond these limits, no edict of theirs can be executed unless it be at our command. . . .

One of the most pernicious effects of this system is to persuade our parlements that their deliberations acquire more weight in consequence of these principles; and already some of them, believing that they have become more powerful or independent, have given currency to maxims that were unknown until recently. They have called themselves 'representatives of the nation, necessary interpreters of the public will of Kings, guardians over the administration of the public services and the settlement of royal debts'; and soon they will acknowledge no virtue in our laws except in so far as they themselves shall have adopted and legalised them; and they will rear up their authority at the side of ours, if not above it, reducing our legislative power to the mere faculty of proposing our desires to them, and reserving to themselves the right to prevent the carrying out of our will.

If after having listened with patience and kindness to their remonstrances, we still feel it our duty to have our laws registered at our command, these courts are seen to rise up against this ancient and legitimate exercise of our power, and they qualify these registrations as *illegal entries*, contrary to what they call *the fundamental principles of the monarchy*. They come away from the court when our messengers begin to carry out our orders. . . . Before proscribing them by our edict, we wish to remind our courts of the principles from which they ought never to depart.

We hold our crown from God alone; the right to make laws for the guidance and government of our subjects does not depend upon anyone else and is not shared with anybody. We address these laws to our courts so that they may be examined, discussed and put into execution; when these courts find certain inconveniences in the terms of these laws, we have accorded to them the permission to make the respectable remonstrances they might judge suitable; we have several times assured them that we would listen to all that they had to say for the good of our subjects and our service. . . .

But this practice . . . does not mean that our officials have a right of resistance; their representations only have a limited validity; it is not they who can out bounds upon our authority. . . .

       F. A. Isambert, *Récueil général*, XXII, pp 501–9, in H. Butterfield, op cit, pp 55–7

Questions

a How far do extracts *a*, *b* and *c* suggest Louis XV's personal inadequacies and incompetent leadership as King?
b Who was 'the late cardinal' mentioned by the Marquis d'Argenson in line 18?
c Was Lord Chesterfield correct in his comments upon the French Church and the parlements (lines 35–9)?
* d Do you agree that the absence of firm control over French policy under Louis XV was especially disastrous in foreign affairs?

3 The Crisis of Louis XVI's Reign

(a) The financial situation

The financial troubles of the monarchy brought matters to a head. The administrative and fiscal structure of the kingdom was grossly obsolete, and . . . the attempt to remedy this by the reforms of 1774–6 failed, defeated by the resistance of vested interests headed by the parlements. Then France became involved in the American War of Independence. Victory over England was obtained at the cost of final bankruptcy, and thus the American Revolution can claim to be the direct cause of the French. Various expedients were tried with diminishing success, but nothing short of a fundamental reform, which mobilized the real and considerable taxable capacity of the country could cope with a situation in which expenditure outran revenue by at least 20 per cent, and no effective economies were possible. For though the extravagance of Versailles has often been blamed for the crisis, court expenditure only amounted to 6 per cent of the total in 1788. War, navy and diplomacy made up one quarter, the service of the existing debt one half. War and debt – the American war and its debt – broke the back of the monarchy.

    E. J. Hobsbawm, *The Age of Revolution 1789–1848* (1964), pp 79–80

(b) The Assembly of Notables, 1787

Unhappily Turgot could continue only twenty months . . . on the very threshold of the business, he proposes that the Clergy, the Noblesse, the very Parlements be subjected to taxes like the People! One shriek of indignation and astonishment reverberates through all the Château galleries; the poor King, who had written a few weeks ago, 'There is none but you and I that has the people's interests at heart', must write now a dismissal.

    . . . And so Necker sustains the burden of the finances, for five years long. . . . His Compte Rendu, published by the royal permission, fresh signs of a New Era, shows wonders. . . . Nay, he too has to produce his scheme of taxing: Clergy, Noblesse to be taxed; Provincial Assemblies and the rest – like a mere Turgot! . . . Let Necker also depart; not unlamented. . . . Nay, in seriousness, let no man say that Colonne had not genius; genius for persuading; before all things for Borrowing . . . but did he not produce something with it, namely peace and prosperity, for the time being? . . . The misery is, such a time cannot last! Squandering and payment by Loan is no way to choke a Deficit . . . (after three years) an expedient, unheard of for these hundred and sixty years, has been propounded . . . a Convocation of Notables . . . on the 22nd Day of February 1787.

    Thomas Carlyle, *The French Revolution* (Ward, Lock, n.d.), pp 48–53

Questions

a Name the position occupied at different times by Turgot, Necker and Callone. What was 'the Château' (line 23)?
b What were the chief 'taxes' to which 'the People' were subjected (line 21)?
c What do extracts *a* and *b* suggest were the reasons for the failure

of reform during the last years of the French monarchy?
* *d* Was the Assembly of Notables 'a tactical defeat for the French Crown' (Stuart Andrews)?

VII Habsburgs and Hohenzollerns

Introduction

The Empress Maria Theresa made efforts to establish a system of centralisation and to improve the administration of the Habsburg lands. The contemporary publicist, Joseph von Sonnenfels (1732–1817), one of the intellectual supporters of reform, wrote an eulogy of her reign and her achievements (p 74 below). Until quite recently her reputation has suffered in comparison with that of her son. She has been regarded as a half-hearted, conservative reformer whose inadequacies were revealed by the bolder measures afterwards undertaken by him. Nowadays, however, historians are asking whether she was rather a real and even determined reformer, who achieved important successes in religious affairs, education, serfdom and law, which prepared the way for Joseph's reforms?

His reforms were along the lines she had set out, but were more rapid and thorough and included the introduction of religious toleration, which she had refused to countenance (p 23 above). As well as measures typical of Enlightened Despotism (p 46 above), he followed a thorough and uncompromising policy of Germanisation (which his mother had unknowingly made easier for him), and the extract on page 75 below contains the reply he made to the protests of a Magyar nobleman about this. He also pursued an ambitious foreign policy. He wished to exchange the Netherlands for Bavaria, but was thwarted by Frederick the Great, who formed the League of Princes against him in 1785. The extract on page 75 below sets out Frederick's reasons for the League.

The Holy Roman Empire was becoming an increasingly shadowy realm for the Habsburgs. When, on 18 May 1804, Napoleon declared himself Emperor of the French, less than three months later Francis II assumed the hereditary title of Emperor of Austria in addition to his elective position as Holy Roman Emperor. The extract on page 77 below is from the letter-patent announcing his decision. And after the Treaty of Pressburg and the formation of the Confederation of the Rhine, Francis issued a declaration (p 78 below) in which he surrendered the title of Holy Roman Emperor.

On 14 October 1806, Napoleon defeated a Prussian force at Jena, and another French army routed the main Prussian army at

Auerstadt. It was the most crushing military disaster Prussia had ever suffered. Two weeks later Berlin fell to Napoleon. The shock of the catastrophe has a stimulating effect in Prussia, most notably upon Johann Gottlieb Fichte. A disciple of the idealist philosopher, Immanuel Kant, he at first supported the French Revolution, but then upheld Prussian nationalism. The extract on page 80 below is taken from the addresses he gave in Berlin in 1807–8 during the French occupation of the city, which helped to inspire the Prussian revival that followed and led to the reorganisation of the state by several soldiers and statesmen. Prince Karl von Hardenburg, as Chancellor (1750–1822) undertook many social and political reforms. He expressed his ideas in a memorandum in 1807 from which there are two extracts on pages 81–2 below.

1 Habsburg Policy under Maria Theresa and Joseph II

(a) Her administrative reforms (1)

On the accession of Maria Theresa, the monarchy had neither external influence nor internal vigour; for ability there was no emulation and no encouragement; the state of agriculture was miserable, trade small, the finances badly managed, and credit bad.
5   At her death, she left to her successor a kingdom improved by her many reforms, and placed in that rank which its size and fertility and the intelligence of its inhabitants ought always to enable it to maintain.

Louis Léger, *A History of Austria–Hungary*, trans., B. Hill (1889), pp 380–1

(b) Her administrative reforms (2)

The Imperial system created by Maria Theresa was strictly Imperial,
10   or even 'Austrian'; it had no national character. Still, the members of the Imperial Chancellery in Vienna and most of the captains of circles were Germans: they received a German education and used German as the language of official business among themselves. They would have been surprised to learn that they were discharging
15   a 'German' mission. All the same, once national spirit stirred, the Germanised bureaucracy gave German nationalism its claim to the inheritance of the Habsburgs; and the Habsburgs themselves came to puzzle over the question whether they were a German dynasty.

A. J. P. Taylor, *The Habsburg Monarchy 1809–1918* (1948), p 16

(c) His policy of Germanisation

Every proposal ought to be based upon the irrefutable arguments of reason. . . . The German language is the universal language of my empire. The principalities which I possess are provinces which form one whole with the state of which I am the head. If the Kingdom of Hungary had been the most important of my possessions, I should not have hesitated to make all the other countries speak Hungarian.

Louis Léger, op cit, p 384

(d) His foreign policy (1)

It was only by a great effort that the aged Frederick [the Great] had contrived during his last years to maintain the position which he had secured for himself and for Prussia. His alliance with Russia had lost its value more and more. Joseph II had virtually displaced him in 1781, and henceforward, secure in his powerful backing, devoted his attention to Austrian power and prestige in Germany. He conceived the plan of extending the Habsburg territories at the expense of Bavaria and compensating the Elector by transferring his rule to Belgium. He also secured the appointment of his brothers as Archbishop Electors, thus increasing his own influence in the Empire, and now ventured to adopt the full demeanour of an Emperor *vis-à-vis* the smaller 'Estates'. Frederick countered these moves by organising the rulers of the medium and smaller states in a League of Princes (1785) for the defence of the Imperial Constitution under the leadership of Prussia; and this achieved its purpose for the time being, for Joseph abandoned his designs on Bavaria. In the following year, however, Frederick passed away.

J. Haller, *The Epochs of German History* (1930), p 171

(e) His foreign policy (2)

Explanation of Frederick II, 1785 – The King, being then persuaded for the above-mentioned reasons that the Court of Vienna has no right to acquire Bavaria by exchange or any other method, but that notwithstanding this, that court, according to all probability, is still often engaged upon this project and believes itself authorised to conclude a *so-called free exchange* – witness its repeated attempts to do this and also the declarations it has spread over the whole of Europe; H.M., being unable for reasons which have been indicated in the same way, to stand indifferent while a neighbouring Power makes an aggrandisement so considerable and at the same time so arbitrary and unjust; having secured a permanent right to oppose it, at the peace of Teschen [1779] and after a war undertaken for the very purpose; as Elector and Prince of the Empire, and as contracting party and guarantor of the treaties of Westphalia and Teschen, both justified and interested in watching and co-operating with all his forces to ensure that the Constitution and equilibrium of the German Empire are completely maintained, and particularly to prevent the expulsion from the Empire of one of the oldest and most illustrious Houses of Germany, whose preservation is essential to the equilibrium of Germany; has felt bound for his own safety and preservation as well as for that of the whole German Empire, to do no less than propose to his illustrious partners in the Empire the formation of an Association. This Association is conformable to the fundamental laws of the Empire and in particular to the peace of Westphalia [1648], to the imperial Capitulations and to the customs of all ages, since it has no other aim but to maintain the present legal constitution of the Empire, to preserve each of its members in the free and peaceful enjoyment of his State, rights and possessions, and to oppose any unjust or arbitrary enterprise. The Most Serene Electors of Saxony and of Brunswick-Lüneburg having manifested the same sentiments, the King, as Elector of Brandenburg, has concluded with them a treaty of union which does not touch on any matters save those that have been presented above, and tends only to the maintenance of the Constitution and System of the Empire; a union which is therefore directed neither against the Emperor nor against the Empire, nor against any of its members; which does not endanger either the rights or the dignity of His Imperial Majesty, and which could not offend or alarm the Court of Vienna if its views and sentiments relative to the German constitution were such as one can expect them to be, or such as we confidently anticipate from the magnanimity and rectitude of its august Chief. . . .

It is believe that convincing proof has been given above of the fact that the union which the King has concluded with the Most Serene Electors of Saxony and Brunswick-Lüneburg is not only innocent and legal, but also useful and necessary for the maintenance of the liberty and security of the Empire and its members. In consequence of this, H.M. feels obliged to bring it to the knowledge of his co-partners in the Empire, and hastens to do so, declaring that he is ready to communicate the whole extent of the scheme to them if they desire it, and leaving it to them to accede if they think fit. There are grounds for expecting them to make this accession, considering their rights and their patriotic sentiments, and H.M. the King the Most Serene Electors of Saxony and Brunswick-Lüneburg will count it a pleasure in this event to receive these states into the union, and let them participate in all the resulting advantages. They will concert with them on this subject and come to an agreement concerning everything that shall be deemed ultimately necessary.

  E. F. Graf von Hertzberg, *Recueil des déductions, manifestes, etc., qui on été rédigés et publiés pour la cour de la Prusse* (3 vols, 1789–95), II, pp 307–10, in H. Butterfield, *Select Documents*, pp 43–5

Questions

a How would exchanging Bavaria for the Netherlands have strengthened both Joseph's policy of Germanisation and the strategic position of the Habsburg lands?
b How did Frederick seek to persuade the German states to accept Prussian leadership against Joseph?
c Who were 'the captains of circles' (line 11)? What was the significance of Frederick's references to the Treaties of Westphalia and Teschen?
* d Was Joseph II right in insisting, when he died, that his failure had been complete?

2 The Habsburgs in a Changing Europe

(a) Francis II becomes Emperor of Austria

11 August 1804 – Although by the grace of God, and the choice of the electors of the Romano-Germanic empire, we have been raised to such a degree of splendour as leaves us no title to desire, nevertheless our solicitude as ruler of the house and monarchy of
5 Austria induces us to insist on the maintenance of complete equality between our imperial title and hereditary dignity, and those of the other sovereigns and illustrious powers of Europe, in such fashion as befits the ancient splendour of our house and the greatness and independence of our kingdoms and principalities. We have,
10 therefore, been induced, after the example of the imperial court of Russia in the last century, and of the new sovereign of France, to claim for the house of Austria an hereditary imperial title for its own states. For these reasons we have determined, after mature deliberation, to take solemnly for ourselves and our successors, for
15 the whole of our kingdoms and lands, the hereditary title of Emperor of Austria after the name of our house. At the same time, we declare that each one of our kingdoms, our principalities, and our provinces shall nevertheless preserve its title, constitution and privileges.

  Louis Léger, op cit, pp 421–2

(b) The Confederation of the Rhine, 1806

I The estates of Their Majesties the Kings of Bavaria and Würtemberg, and of Their Serene Highnesses the Elector Arch-Chancellor, the Elector of Baden, the Duke of Berg and Cleves, the Landgrave of Hesse-Darmstadt, etc., etc., . . . shall be for ever separated from the territory of the German Empire and shall combine in a special confederation called the Confederation of the Rhine.

II Any law of the German Empire which has hitherto concerned and applied to Their Majesties and Their Serene Highnesses the Kings, Princes and the Count named in the preceding article, or their subjects or states, or any part of them, shall be declared void and of no effect relative to their said Majesties and Highnesses and the said Count. . . .

III Each of the Kings and Princes in the Confederation will renounce those of his titles which denote any kind of connection with the German Empire; and on the first of August next he will make an announcement to the Diet of his separation from the Empire.

> Georges Fréderic de Martens, *Supplement au recueil des principaux traités* (4 vols, 1802–18), IV, pp 313–26, in H. Butterfield, op cit, pp 85–6

(c) The dissolution of the Holy Roman Empire, 1806

6 August 1806 – Since the Peace of Pressburg [1805] all our care and attention has been directed towards the scrupulous fulfilment of all engagements contracted by the said treaty, as well as the preservation of peace, so essential to the happiness of our subjects, and the strengthening in every way of the friendly relations which have happily been re-established. We could but await the outcome of events in order to determine whether the important changes in the German Empire resulting from the terms of the peace would allow us to fulfill the weighty duties which, in view of the conditions of our election, devolve upon us as the head of the Empire. But the results of certain articles of the Treaty of Pressburg, which showed themselves immediately after its publication and since that time, as well as the events which, as is generally known, have taken place in the German Empire, have convinced us that it would be impossible under these circumstances further to fulfill the duties which we assumed by the conditions of our election. Even if the prompt readjustment of existing political complications might produce an alteration in the existing conditions, the convention signed at Paris, July 12, and approved later by the contracting parties, providing for the complete separation of several important states of the Empire and their union into a separate Confederation, would utterly destroy any such hope.

Thus convinced of the utter impossibility of longer fulfilling the duties of our Imperial office, we owe it to our principles and to our honour to renounce a crown which could only retain value in our eyes so long as we were in a position to justify the confidence reposed in us by the electors, princes, estates, and other members of the German Empire, and to fulfill the duties devolving upon us.

We proclaim, accordingly, that we consider the ties which have hitherto united us to the body politic of the German Empire as hereby dissolved; that we regard the office and dignity of the Imperial headship as extinguished by the formation of a separate union of the Rhenish states, and regard ourselves as thereby freed from all our obligations toward the German Empire; herewith laying down the Imperial crown which is associated with these obligations, and relinquishing the Imperial government which we have hitherto conducted.

We free at the same time the electors, princes, and estates, and all others belonging to the Empire, particularly the members of the Supreme Imperial Courts and other magistrates of the Empire, from the duties constitutionally due to us as the lawful head of the Empire. Conversely, we free all our German provinces and Imperial lands from all their obligations of whatever kind toward the German Empire. In uniting these, as Emperor of Austria, with the whole body of the Austrian state we shall strive, with the restored and existing peaceful relations with all the powers and neighbouring states, to raise them to the height of prosperity and happiness which is our keenest desire and the aim of our constant and sincerest efforts.

J. Meyer, *Corpus juris confoederationis Germanicae* (2nd edn, i, p 107) in J. H. Robinson, *Readings in European History*, II pp 501–3

Questions

a Explain 'the example of the imperial court of Russia in the last century and of the new sovereign of France' (line 10) which led Francis to proclaim himself Emperor of Austria.
b What were the 'Supreme Imperial Courts' (line 77)?
c How had the Peace of Pressburg (line 38) affected the Holy Roman Empire?
★ d Do you agree that Napoleon's creation of the Confederation of the Rhine prepared the way for German unity?

3 The Reorganisation of Prussia

(a) Fichte's call

In this belief [in the uniqueness and truth of an individual culture] our earliest common forefathers . . . the Germanii, as the Romans called them, bravely resisted the oncoming world domination of the Romans. Did they not have before their eyes the greater
5 brilliance of the Roman provinces next to them and the more refined enjoyments. . . . Were not the Romans willing enough to let them share in all these blessings? To those who submitted the Romans gave marks of distinction in the form of kingly titles, high commands in their armies and Roman orders. . . . Had they no
10 appreciation of the advantages of Roman civilisation, e.g. of the superior organisation of the armies, in which even an Arminius [the German tribal leader who defeated the Romans in AD 9] did not disdain to learn the trade of war? They cannot be charged with ignorance or lack of consideration of any of these. Their
15 descendants, as soon as they could do so without losing their freedom, even assimilated Roman culture, so far as this was possible without losing their individuality. Why then did they fight for several generations in bloody wars that broke out again and again with ever-renewed force? A Roman writer puts the following
20 expression into the mouths of their leaders: '*What was left for them to do, except to maintain their freedom or else to die before they became slaves?*' Freedom to them meant just this: remaining Germans and continuing to settle their own affairs, independently and in accordance with the original spirit of their race, going on with their
25 development in accordance with the same spirit, and propagating this independence in their posterity. All these blessings which the Romans offered meant slavery to them because then they would have to become something which was not German, they would have to become half-Roman. They assumed as a matter of course
30 that every man would rather die than become half a Roman and that a true German would only want to live in order to be, and to remain, just a German, and to bring up his children as Germans.

They did not all die; they did not see slavery; they bequeathed freedom to their children. It is their unyielding resistance which
35 the whole modern world has to thank for being what it now is. Had the Romans succeeded in bringing them also under the yoke and in destroying them as a nation, which the Romans did in every case, the whole development of the human race would have taken a different course. . . .

        Johann Gottlieb Fichte, *Addresses to the German Nation*, trans. R. F. Jones and G. H. Turnbull (1922), pp 143–5

(b) Fichte's influence

The German nation, it is scarcely too much to say, discovered itself by contrast with the French and through loathing of them. Distance alone lent enchantment to the German view of the French. Early enthusiasts later turned haters; a transformation facilitated, of course, by the Revolution's simultaneous turning into the Empire. West and south-west German simmerings before 1806, Napoleon managed to suppress. It was beyond his power to stop the spread and the boiling once his troops and collectors had got to Vienna and Berlin. All he could do was to intimidate the Germans from thoughts of armed insurgency, and to compel the suppression of sentiments too overtly anti-French. . . . Among the earliest of these, as it has remained one of the most enduring, was Fichte's series of public lectures given in Berlin through the winter of 1807–8 and immediately published under the title *Addresses to the German Nation*. There was nothing in them explicitly about military revival. They were about the national revival which – it could be understood – must precede it. Searching about almost frantically for explanations of their upset, Prussia's rulers were ready to listen to voices they had hitherto on the whole ignored. The reformers seized their opportunity. Nothing less than total structural change would suffice. Army and society had to move together. Only a people feeling themselves to be free men could fight hard enough to sustain a free state.

Geoffrey Best, *War and Society in Revolutionary Europe 1770–1870* (1982), pp 155–6

(c) Von Hardenburg on the Nobility

(1) Let every office in the State without exception be open not to this or that caste, but to merit, ability and capability from all classes. Let every office be the object of general emulation, and let no man's energy, be he ever so insignificant, ever so mean, be ruled by the thought: 'The keenest enthusiasm and the greatest activity will never fit you for it, or make you attain it.' Let no power be checked in its struggle for good.

(2) The exclusive privilege of the nobility to the possession of so-called manorial properties is . . . so injurious, and now so little in keeping with our times and constitutions, that its abolition is a matter of absolute necessity, as is that of all other advantages, which the laws have so far alone accorded to the noble or landed proprietor. . . .

(3) In regard to the freedom of taxation, many important considerations present themselves. Absolute authority ought, from many reasons, to exist in this also. The nobility no longer perform

the services, for which they remained exempt, uncompensated, but on the contrary at considerable expense (to the State). Justice demands their participation in the burthens of the State and the equal distribution of those burthens.

> Karl von Hardenburg, *Memorandum*, 1807, *Denkwurdigkeiten des Staatskanslers von Hardenburg*, 1877, in E. Reich, *Select Documents*, pp 571–2

(d) Von Hardenburg on the peasantry

The most numerous and important estate of the realm, although hitherto the most neglected and oppressed, the Peasantry, must necessarily be an especial object of our care. The abolition of hereditary serfdom should, once and for all, be enacted by law. Likewise the statutes by which the peasant is impeded from leaving the peasant estate should be repealed. The military organisation will not suffer thereby, if right measures are taken. Let the acquisition of property by peasants be facilitated, whether as regards new acquisitions or in the redemption of the rights of the lord of the manor. It is not requisite to abolish compulsory labour. Frequently it is not only not burthensome, but often more advantageous to those upon whom it falls, than a pecuniary one.

Modifications in this respect should be left to voluntary agreement, and only furthered by laws, in so far as the principles be fixed, according to which services *in natura* (not in money) can be redeemed. By strict regulations a check must be set upon arbitrary power and upon the oppressor. The most important and most injurious oppression is caused by military and other purveyances, because the peasant is compelled to keep more draught animals than he needs for uncertain services; because he is often interrupted for several days in his work and compelled to be absent from his farm; finally because this burthen is unevenly distributed over the land.

> Ibid.

Questions

a   What was Fichte's message for his contemporaries when he spoke about the resistance of the Germans to the ancient Romans?

b   What were 'hereditary serfdom' (line 86) and 'services in *natura*' (line 97)?

c   How would the reforms wanted by Von Hardenburg in extracts c and d be likely to improve Prussia's military effectiveness?

★ d   In what ways had the Hohenzollerns become leaders of German nationalism by 1815?

VIII Russia and its Neighbours

Introduction

While serfdom was disappearing in western Europe, it remained in Russia and was very onerous for a large part of the peasantry. The extracts on pages 84–5 below contain advertisements in the *Moskovskie Vedomsti* (*Moscow Times*), words spoken by a Russian landlord to his serfs and an account by a Frenchman in Russia, who observed the way in which serfdom degraded both landowner and serf.

The Charter of Nobility issued by Catherine the Great in 1785 (p 85 below) has been commonly regarded as being issued solely for the advantage of the landowners, but recently it has been represented as part of her policy of sustaining and strengthening the nobility, by recognising them as a separate estate with particular rights and privileges, who would be able to lead Russian society away from its prevailing cultural isolation and economic backwardness. She adopted the same attitude towards the barely established middle class, whose composition and position is described on page 86 below by William Coxe, later Archdeacon of Wiltshire, who went to the country as a travelling tutor in 1778–9.

The westernising reforms introduced in the reign of Peter the Great (1682–1725) mostly survived after his death, despite the series of mediocre rulers who followed him on the Russian throne. During the years until Catherine's accession in 1762, the throne changed hands six times, and on each occasion the succession was resolved by the imperial guards. She gained the crown by the last such palace revolution of the century. Her reign of thirty-four years brought stability at last to the dynasty.

Catherine's reign was notable in foreign affairs for the three partitions of Poland (1771, 1793 and 1795). The extracts on pages 90–1 below from the Preambles to the First and Third Partition Treaties contain the reasons put forward by Russia, Prussia and Austria for their action in dividing Poland between themselves. Catherine engaged in the First Partition on Frederick the Great's initiative, but she herself inspired and dominated both the later ones. Russia gained the largest share of territory from Poland's extinction.

More than Poland, the territory of the Turkish Empire in the region of the Balkans and the Black Sea attracted Catherine's ambitions. The Russo-Turkish War of 1768–74 ended with the Treaty of Kuchuk Kainardji, which Frederick said was the result not so much of Russian military prowess as of Turkish incompetence and imbecility. Its importance for Russia lay in political control rather than territorial gains. It may be said to mark the beginning of the Eastern Question, which was concerned with the problems raised by the decay of the Turkish Empire and the fear of Russian exploitation of this on the part of the other European powers. Catherine's dreams of empire-building in the Balkans foreshadowed the future direction of Russian policy, but the British Ambassador's letters of 1779 (p 94 below) showed that he was not alarmed by them.

1   The Social Classes

(a) Serfs – for sale

For sale: domestics and skilled craftsmen of good behaviour, viz. two tailors, a shoemaker, a watchmaker, a cook, a coachmaker, a wheelwright, an engraver, a gilder and coach-men, who may be inspected and their price ascertained in the 4th district, Section 3,
5   at the proprietor's own house, No 15. Also for sale are three young racehorses, one colt and two geldings and a pack of hounds, fifty in number, which will be a year old in January and February next.

In District 12, a maid of sixteen for sale, able to weave lace, sew linen, do ironing and starching and to dress her mistress;
10   furthermore, has a pleasing face and figure.

Ian Grey, *Catherine the Great* (1961), p 122

(b) The serfs – their owner

I am your lord, and my lord is the Czar. The Czar has a right to give me orders, and I must obey, but not to give them to you. On my estate I am the Czar, I am your God on earth, and I must be responsible for you to God in heaven. . . . First a horse must be
15   curried ten times with the iron curry-comb, then only can you brush it with the soft brush. I shall have to curry you pretty roughly, and who knows whether I shall ever get down to the brush. God cleanses the air with thunder and lightening, and in my village I shall cleanse with thunder and fire, whenever I think
20   it necessary.

A. von Haxthausen, *Studien . . . ueber Russland* (2 vols, 1847), II, p 3, in E. J. Hobsbawm, *The Age of Revolution 1789–1848* (1962), p 180

84   EIGHTEENTH-CENTURY EUROPE

(c) The serfs – their treatment

What has disgusted me is to see men, with grey hair and patriarchal beards, lying on their faces, with their breeches down, flogged like children. Still more horrible! – I blush to write it – there are masters who sometimes force the son to inflict this punishment on his father; and, most abominable of all, there are sons who comply with such an insult. These and many other horrid actions are committed chiefly in the country, where the lords, in their castles, exercise the same authority over men as over animals. Even women are subjected to the most indelicate insults.

C. F. Mason, *Secret Memoirs of the Court of St Petersburg*, trans. H. S. Nichols (1895), p 284

(d) The nobility – Catherine's Charter of the Nobility, 1785

1 The noble calling is the result, rising out of the qualities and virtues of men who held high office in the past, and distinguished themselves by their merits, by which they transformed the service itself into a dignity, and won for their descendants the noble appellation.

2 It is not only useful for the empire and the throne, but also just, to preserve and firmly establish the honourable estate of the well-born nobility; and hence the dignity of nobility shall remain inalienable from oldest times to the present, and for all time by inheritance to the descendants of those families that now enjoy it, as follows:

3 The nobleman transmits his noble status to his wife.

4 The nobleman transmits his well-born noble status by inheritance to his children.

8 Without judicial proceedings no well-born person can lose noble status.

10 Without judicial proceedings no well-born person can lose his life.

11 Without judicial proceedings no well-born person can lose his property.

12 The well-born person can be judged only by his peers.

15 Corporal punishment may not be inflicted on any well-born person.

16 Noblemen serving in the lower ranks of our Army shall be liable only to such punishments as our military regulations prescribe for higher officers.

17 We guarantee freedom and independence to the Russian nobility for all time, by inheritance in future generations.

20 [Duty of nobles to defend the state.]

26 Well-born persons are confirmed in the right to purchase villages.

27 Well-born persons are confirmed in the right to sell at wholesale what has been harvested in their villages or produced by handicraft.

28 Well-born persons are permitted to have manufactories and industrial works in their villages.

30 Well-born persons are confirmed in their right to possess, build or buy houses in the cities, and to carry on manufacturing enterprises therein.

32 Well-born persons are permitted to sell products raised on their estates at wholesale overseas or to have them exported through the designated ports. . . .

33 Well-born persons . . . are confirmed in the right to possess, not only the surface of the lands belonging to them, but also whatever minerals or plants may be present in the depths beneath the soil or waters, and likewise all metals extracted therefrom. . . .

34 Well-born persons are confirmed in the right to possess the forests on their estates, and in the right of free use of these forests. . . .

35 In the villages the house of the lord shall be exempt from military quartering.

36 The well-born person is himself freed from personal taxes.

R. R. Palmer, *The Age of Democratic Revolution* (2 vols, 1959), II, pp 508–9

(e) The middle classes – observations of an English traveller

Peter, who during his travels, perceived the utility of a third estate for the purposes of commerce, made many regulations with this view, which, though excellent in themselves, yet not being adapted to the state of property in Russia, did not answer to the end proposed. Among these regulations, he endowed some free towns with certain privileges, which were afterwards augmented by Elizabeth. But these privileges were confined to Petersburgh, Moscow, Astracan, Tver, and a few other great provincial towns; and all the inhabitants, even merchants not excepted, were not distinguished from the peasants, in two instances, which are considered in this country as indelible marks of servitude: they were subject to the poll-tax and to be drafted for the army and navy. Catherine has exempted the body of merchants from these two instances of servitude, has increased the number and immunities of the free towns, and permitted many of the crown-peasants and all free men, to enrol themselves, under stipulated conditions, in the class of merchants or burghers.

The merchants are distributed into three classes. The first comprehends those who have a capital of 10 000 roubles; the second those who possess 5 000; and the third, those who are worth

500. ... All persons who choose to enter themselves in any of these classes are exempted from the poll-tax, on condition of paying annually one per cent of their capital employed in trade to the crown. ...

This alteration in the mode of assessing merchants is advantageous both to the crown and to the subjects; the former receives, and the latter cheerfully pay, one per cent of their capital, because they are exempted from the poll-tax, and are entitled to additional immunities. It is also a just impost, as each merchant pays according to his fortune. ... With respect to the general interests of the nation, it is a masterpiece of policy; it excites industry, by holding up to the people a principle of honour, as well as of interest, to be derived from the augmentation of their capital; and affords an additional security from arbitrary impositions, by pledging the good faith of government in the protection of their property. It is likewise productive of another essential public benefit by creating, as it were, a third estate, which, as it increases in wealth, credit and importance, must by degrees acquire additional privileges and gradually rise into consequence.

The burghers form the second division of this order: the term burgher is applied to all inhabitants of free towns, who declare that they possess a capital of less than £100. ... They possess many privileges superior to the peasants; but are distinguished from the merchants by being still subject to the poll-tax and to enrolment in the army or navy.

Under the third order must be included all the other free subjects of the empire; namely, those slaves who have received liberty from their masters; those who have obtained their dismission from the army and navy; the Members of the Academy of Arts, and of other similar institutions, ... and, lastly, the children of all those freemen. All these persons have permission to settle and trade in any part of the empire and may enrol themselves according to the capital, among the burghers or merchants. By these wise regulations, the number of persons above slaves will gradually increase and must in time form a very considerable order of men, as soon as they shall acquire the right of possessing land.

> William Coxe, *Travels in Poland, Russia, Sweden and Denmark* (1779), in Peter Putnam, *Seven Britons in Imperial Russia 1698–1812* (1952), pp 270–3

Questions

a What does extract *d* suggest were Catherine's motives in issuing the Charter of Nobility?
b Who were 'well-born persons' (line 50) and 'crown-peasants' (line 96)? What were 'servitude' (line 92) and the 'poll-tax' (line 93)?
c What was the purpose of the Russian government in dividing

the merchants into three classes as described in extract *e*?

* *d* 'In the eighteenth century the power of the central government in Russia was limited in practice by the sheer physical difficulty of enforcing its commands over such a vast area' (M. S. Anderson). Do you think that this was the main reason for the difficulties faced by Catherine in securing the adoption of her policies?

2   The Reign of Catherine II (1762–96)

(a) Her seizure of power

The new empress was even less Russian than Peter. Sophia of Anhalt-Zerbst, who had been renamed Catherine on her reception into the Russian Orthodox Church, was the daughter of a Prussian noble family. In 1745 she became the bride of Peter, at that time
5 heir to the throne, as part of one of Frederick the Great's diplomatic manoeuvres.

Catherine's early years in Russia were dangerous and difficult, and on occasion she was almost caught in the web of intrigue and counter-intrigue that characterised Elizabeth's reign. In this hard
10 school she learned political realism. Unlike Peter, she adopted Russian manners, learned the language and professed Orthodoxy. When her hour struck, she was able to put herself forward as the representative of the Russian people, Orthodoxy and the army. First Peter, then Ivan IV (who had survived in confinement since
15 1741) were murdered, and Catherine was able to remain the undisputed ruler of Russia until her death in 1796.

Nathaniel Harris, *Struggle for Supremacy* (1969), p 65

(b) Her Proclamation of 1762

By the Grace of God, we, Catherine the Second, Empress and Autocrat of All Russia, etc., etc.

To all true sons of the Russian Fatherland it has been clear what
20 danger has indeed begun to threaten the Russian nation: And namely our Orthodox Church has awaken to the dangers to our ecclesiastical traditions, through which our Greek Church has been subjected to the final threat of the transformation of ancient orthodoxy in Russia and the adoption of a foreign rite. Secondly,
25 Russian prestige, raised so high by our victorious army at the price of shedding so much blood, has been completely degraded by the conclusion of a new peace with the enemy himself. At the same time the internal government, on which the unity and welfare of our whole Fatherland rests, has been completely overthrown.
30 Therefore, convinced of the danger threatening all our loyal

subjects, we have felt compelled, calling God and His Justice to our aid, and especially conscious that it is the clear and honest desire of all our loyal subjects, to ascend the throne as All-Russian Autocrat, whereupon all our true subjects have sworn the solemn
35 oath of allegiance. Catherine.
Princess E. R. Dashkova, *Memoirs*, trans. and ed. Kuril Fitzlyon (1958), p 31

(c) The British Ambassador's portrait of her, 1765

Much stress is laid upon her resolution, particularly in the instance of dethroning her husband. Desperate situations make cowards valiant. She was compelled either to ruin him or submit herself to that confinement which she knew had long been in deliberation.
40 Those who know her well say she is rather enterprising than brave, and that her appearance of courage arouses some time from a conviction of the pusillanimity of her enemies, at others from her not seeing her danger. She is certainly bolder than the generality of her sex. . . .
45 Those who are most in her society assure me that her application to business is incredible. The welfare and prosperity of her subjects, the glory of her empire, are always present to her; and to all appearance her care will raise the reputation and power of Russia to a point which, at present, they have never reached, if she does
50 not indulge too much in far-fetched and unpractical theories, which interested or ignorant people are too ready to suggest to her. Her foible is to be too systematic, and that may be the rock on which she may, perhaps, split. She embraces too many objects at once; she likes to begin, regulate and correct projects all in a moment.
55 Indefatigable in everything she undertakes, she obliges her ministers to work incessantly. They argue, make plans and sketch out a thousand schemes, and decide upon nothing. Among those who hold the first rank in her confidence, some will be found who have experience, but few if any who possess superior talents.
The Despatches and Correspondence of John Hobart, Second Earl of Buckingham (Camden Soc., 2 vols), I, pp 100–2

Questions

a Explain these statements – 'she was almost caught in the web of intrigue and counter-intrigue that characterised Elizabeth's reign' (line 8) and 'she was compelled either to ruin him or submit herself to that confinement which she knew had long been in deliberation' (line 38).

b What can be learnt from extracts *a* and *c* about Catherine's character and ability?

- c How far do extracts *a* and *b* suggest why Catherine was able to succeed in supplementing Paul III on the Russian throne?
- * d She reversed the trend of eighteenth-century Russian history and returned to the methods of Peter the Great (E. N. Williams). Discuss this verdict upon Catherine II.

3 The Partition of Poland

(a) Poland's fate

Catherine's gains at Poland's expense . . . were shattering for the defeated country. Firstly, in 1763, Russian troops invaded the Duchy of Courland, a fief of Poland, with ice-free ports, which was henceforth treated as Russian territory. Secondly, after the
5 death of Augustus III (1763), the Polish nobles were forced to elect yet another Russian nominee as king: Catherine's former lover, Count Staminas Poniatowski. Thirdly, when this monarch tried to give the Polish central government some semblance of effectiveness (by introducing hereditary kingship and reducing the ways in which
10 the nobility could hamstring the crown), Russia intervened, and in a Russo-Polish treaty the unworkable Polish constitution was placed under Russian guarantee 'for all time to come' (1768). Fourthly, came the three partitions of Poland (1772, 1793 and 1795), whereby as a result of annexation by Russia in league with Prussia and
15 Austria, Poland almost disappeared from the map. Through the wasting disease of the constitution, one of the largest states in Europe had become one of the weakest.

E. N. Williams, *The Ancien Régime in Europe* (1792), p 256

(b) The First Partition, 1772

The Preamble to the Partition Treaty of 25 July 1772 – The spirit of faction, the troubles and internal warfare which have distracted the
20 kingdom of Poland for so many years, and the anarchy which daily acquires new strength there, to the point of destroying the whole authority of established government, arouse just apprehensions that the complete collapse of the state is near, which will upset the relative interests of neighbouring states, destroy the good relations
25 which exist between them and kindle a general war, as already indeed there has arisen from these troubles alone that which Her Majesty the Empress of All the Russias is waging against the Ottoman Porte; and at the same time the powers adjacent to Poland have claims and rights as ancient as they are legitimate, which they
30 have never been able to assert and which they risk losing beyond recall, if they themselves do not take means to assert and establish them, together with the re-establishment of tranquillity and good

order in the interior of this Republic, so giving it a political life more in conformity with the interests of its neighbours. . . .
    G. F. de Martens, *Recueil des principaux Traites*, II, pp 89f.

(c) The Third Partition, 1795

The Preamble to the Partition Treaty of 24 October 1795 – H.M. the Empress has been obliged to take the measures for the repression and extinction of the revolt and insurrection which have broken out in Poland, the results of which are bound to be the most pernicious and dangerous to the tranquillity of the Powers neighbouring upon this state. Her efforts have been crowned with the most happy and complete success, and Poland has been entirely brought into subjection and conquered by the armies of the Empress. Her Majesty, who had been authorised to count upon this issue through a confidence founded upon the justice of her cause and the strength of the preparations she had made to bring it to victory, has hastened to confer in advance with her two Allies, namely H.M. the Holy Roman Emperor and H.M. the King of Prussia, concerning the most effectual measures to be taken for preventing the recurrence of disturbances like those which had given her such justifiable alarm, the seeds of which, forever stirring in minds permeated with the most perverse principles, would not fail to germinate afresh sooner or later, if precautions were not taken by a strong and vigorous government. These two Sovereigns, convinced by their experience in the past that the Republic of Poland is absolutely incapable of providing itself with such a government, or of living peaceably under its laws, and at the same time of keeping itself in any sort of independence, having recognised in their wisdom and in regard for peace and the welfare of their subjects, that it was absolutely necessary to resort and proceed to a total partition of this Republic between the three neighbouring Powers. Being informed of this attitude to the problem, and finding it perfectly analogous to her own, H.I.M. of all the Russias resolved to treat without delay, first of all with each of her above-mentioned Allies separately, and then with both of them together, in order to bring about a final arrangement with respect to the shares which shall fall to each in pursuance of their common determination.
    G. F. de Martens, op cit, VI, p 699, in H. Butterfield, *Select Documents*, pp 38–9

Questions

a Explain these phrases – 'hamstring the crown' (line 10) and 'the wasting disease of the constitution' (line 16).
b What was the connection between the war waged by Catherine

against Turkey (line 26) and the First Partition of Poland?
- c What were the 'disturbances' mentioned in extract c?
* d Did Poland's geographical position make its continuance as an independent state impossible?

4 The Eastern Question

(a) The Treaty of Kuchuk Kainarji, 1774

Art. VII The Sublime Porte promises always to protect the Christian religion and its churches; and also it permits ministers of the imperial court of Russia to make representations on all occasions both in favour of the new church at Constantinople of which there
5 is mention in Article XIV, and in favour of those who serve it; promising to take these representations into consideration, as made by a person of confidence on behalf of a neighbouring and sincerely friendly Power.

Art. VIII It shall be free and allowable to the subjects of the
10 Russian Empire, both lay and clerical, to visit the holy city of Jerusalem and other places worthy of attention. There shall not be exacted from these pilgrims and travellers by anybody either at Jerusalem or elsewhere, any *charatsch*, contribution, duty or other tax; but they shall be furnished with passports and firmans, such
15 as are given to the subjects of other friendly Powers. During their stay in the Ottoman Empire there shall not be the least wrong or injury done to them, but on the contrary they shall be under the most rigid protection of the laws.

Art. XI For the convenience and advantage of the two empires
20 there shall be free and unobstructed navigation for the merchant-ships belonging to the two contracting Powers in all the seas which bathe their lands; the Sublime Porte grants to Russian merchant-ships in particular, such as those which the other Powers use everywhere for commerce and in the ports, a free passage from the
25 Black Sea into the White [Aegean] Sea and reciprocally from the White Sea into the Black Sea; as also to enter all the ports and harbours existing either on the coasts of the sea or in the passages and canals which join these seas. Similarly the Sublime Porte allows Russian subjects to trade by land in its states as well as by sea, and
30 also allows their ships on the Danube, conformably to what is specified above in this article, and this with the same privileges and advantages as are enjoyed by the nations the most friendly to the Porte and the most favoured in matters of commerce, the French and English, for example; and the capitulations of these two nations
35 and others shall serve as the rule in everything and in every place as regards Russian trade and traders, as though they were inserted here word for word; so that Russian traders paying the same dues may import and export all kinds of goods and enter all the

ports and harbours both in the Black Sea and in the other seas, Constantinople being expressly included. . . .

Art. XVI The Russian Empire restores to the Sublime Porte all Bessarabia. . . . the two principalities of Wallachia and Moldavia, with all the fortresses, towns, burgs, villages and everything they contain, and the Sublime Porte receives them on the following conditions, with the solemn promise to observe them sacredly: 1. To grant an eternal and absolute amnesty to all the inhabitants of these principalities, of whatever dignity, rank, estate, vocation or extraction they may be, without the least exception. . . . 2. Not in any way to hinder the free exercise of the Christian religion or to place any obstacle against the construction of new churches or the repair of old ones, as has been the case before. 3. To restore to convents and private persons the lands and possessions hitherto belonging to them. . . . 4. To have for the clergy the special regard which their estate demands. . . . 9. The Porte allows the princes of both these two states to have in Constantinople a *chargé d'affaires*, taken from the Christians of the Greek communion, who shall watch over the matters concerning the said principalities and shall be treated with kindness by the Porte, and who, notwithstanding their lack of importance, shall be considered as persons enjoying the rights of international law, that is to say having immunity from all violence. 10. The Porte consents also that in accordance as in the circumstances of these two principalities might demand it, the ministers of the imperial court of Russia residing in Constantinople may make representations on their behalf; and the Porte promises to hear these representations with the regard that is due to friendly and respected powers.

G. F. D. de Martens, op cit, II, pp 287–322, in H. Butterfield, *Selected Documents*, pp 172–4

(b) The importance of the Treaty

The Treaty of Kuchuk Kainarji was to be of great importance in the history of eastern Europe. Turkey was now shown to be in a moribund condition, unable to uphold the frontiers of her extended empire by her own strength. Russia, having secured her frontier in the west and fastened her grip upon Poland, could take advantage of Turkish weakness and strive to establish her preponderance in eastern Europe. Already she had revealed the way she would do this – by military action combined with intervention in Turkish affairs on behalf of the Orthodox Christians. The Treaty of Kuchuk Kainarji, therefore, may be regarded as marking the beginning of the Eastern Question – the problem of the decline of the Turkish Empire and the expansionist policy of Russia which was to trouble

Europe for more than a century and contribute much to the situation leading to the outbreak of war in 1914.
Leonard W. Cowie, *Eighteenth-Century Europe* (1963), p 271

(c) Catherine's ambitions after the Treaty

Sir James Harris, British Ambassador at St Petersburg, to Viscount Weymouth, Secretary of State, 4 June 1779 – Prince Potemkin himself pays little regard to the politics on the West of Russia; his mind is continually occupied with the idea of raising an Empire in the East; he has so far infected the Empress with these sentiments that she has been chimerical enough to christen the new-born Grand Duke, Constantine; to give him a Greek nurse, whose name was Helen, and to talk in her private society of placing him on the throne of the Eastern Empire. In the meanwhile, she is building a town at Tsarskoe Selo, to be called Constantingorod.

. . .

The present reigning idea (and it carries away all others) is the establishing of a new Empire in the East, at Athens or Constantinople. The Empress discoursed a long while with me the other day on the ancient Greeks, of their alacrity and the superiority of their genius, and the same character being still extant in the modern ones, and of the possibility of their again becoming the first people if properly assisted and seconded. . . . If H.M. should stand in indispensable need of assistance from this quarter [i.e. Russia] the only means of obtaining it is by encouraging this romantic idea. She is now so warmly bent on it, that such a conduct, dexterously managed would give us the firmest hold of this Court; and as its execution, whenever seriously planned, would instantly appear impracticable, we need not be apprehensive of having engaged ourselves too far in an unpleasant transaction.
James Harris, First Earl of Malmesbury, *Diaries and Correspondence* (4 vols, 1844), I, pp 236–8

Questions

a   Indicate the opportunities the Treaty of Kuchuk Kainarji gave Russia to follow the policy outlined in extract *b*.
b   What were the 'Sublime Porte' (line 1) and 'the capitulations' (line 34)?
c   Had Catherine a former empire in mind when she spoke about establishing an 'Eastern Empire' under Russian control (extract *c*)?
★ d   Had Russia become a prominent European power by 1815?

IX   The French Revolution

Introduction

The cataclysmic collapse of the regime in France, the greatest of the states in eighteenth-century Europe, immediately led contemporaries to seek to discover reasons for this unprecedented event, and this has been continued by their successors ever since. No aspect of eighteenth-century European history has been the object of such discussion and research as the French Revolution. Its origins, outcome and significance have long occupied historians, though the difference between the outlook of earlier writers and those of to-day is very great.

The French writer and politician, Alexis de Tocqueville, was the first important historian to attempt an analysis rather than a narrative of the Revolution. He argued in 1856 that its underlying cause was the 'administrative revolution', already in progress under Louis XVI, which made feudal, social and political survivals increasingly onerous and intolerable to the mass of the population. This view was shared by Louis Madelin in 1911, who regarded it as a reaction against the anarchy of the *ancien régime*.

Important among the material for such judgements have been the *cahiers de doléances*, especially those of the third estate. And, indeed, an important trend in the work of recent historians has been the development of the study of French local history. This has resulted in the production of studies of life in the provinces or geographical regions during the eighteenth century, which have added considerably to the knowledge of conditions under the monarchy.

Both French and English historians have debated the significance of the Revolution, from François Mignet and Lord Acton in the nineteenth century to Alphonse Aulard at the turn of the century and Jacob L. Talmon in 1952. Nowadays they are criticised for their concentration upon constitutional and governmental matters, ignorance of events beyond Paris and frequent political bias. Nevertheless, their way of looking at the Revolution as a whole has exercised a lasting influence upon historians. The first to challenge this was Alfred Cobban, and the process he began, though his ideas are not always now supported, has continued.

A recent historian, D. G. M. Sutherland in his *France 1789–*

1815 (1985) has stated that the course of the Revolution 'can be understood as the struggle against a counter-revolution that was not so much aristocratic as massive, extensive, durable and popular'; and he has gone on to say that this affords an explanation 'why the revolutionaries violated their own rule of law with scarcely a qualm'. The recourse to oppression, which this involved, was most vividly displayed in the Terror and most spectacularly in its prominent figure, Robespierre, whose motives and character have constantly been assessed and reassessed. So too have the origins and nature of the Terror itself. Can it be explained, as the British politician, Charles James Fox, insisted (p 102 below), by the danger to the existence of the Republic posed by the allies fighting against France? Or was it due to the increasing innate violence and bloodshed that marked the course of the Revolution?

When the Thermidoreans overthrew the Terror in 1794, they faced problems which were to contribute towards their downfall. These were partly political and partly religious. Those who had suffered in person or family from the Terror demanded revenge. Opposition to the policy of dechristianisation continued. The most immediate of these problems, however, was the threatened collapse of the economy. The last extract in this Section (p 103 below) concerns the misery in Paris produced by this situation which was not, however, confined to the capital.

1 Prelude to Revolution

(a) *The expectations of the people*

It is not always by going from bad to worse that a society falls into revolution. It happens most often that a people, which has supported without complaint, as if they were not felt, the most oppressive laws, violently throws them off as soon as their weight
5 is lightened. The social order destroyed by a revolution is almost always better than that which immediately preceded it, and experience shows that the most dangerous moment for a bad government is generally that in which it sets about reform. . . . Feudalism at the height of its power had not inspired Frenchmen with so much
10 hatred as it did on the eve of its disappearing. The slightest acts of arbitrary power under Louis XVI seemed less easy to endure than all the despotism of Louis XIV.

      A. de Tocqueville, *L'Ancien Régime* (Eng. trans., 1937), p 186

(b) Escape from anarchy

The Revolution of 1789 had been the work of the nation. The 'progress of knowledge' had opened the eyes of the upper classes to the abuses of inequality. The excess of the public suffering had driven the popular classes into rebellion. Their firm resolve to abolish the feudal system had stirred the peasants to revolt. The evident anarchy existing in the King's government had aroused a general desire for a *Constitution*, but by the word Constitution nine-tenths of the French nation understood something more than a charter which should reorganise the State. *Equality in matters of justice and taxation – the abolition of the feudal system – a methodical and orderly system of government* – these were what the Frenchmen of January 1789 sought to obtain.

Louis Madelin, *The French Revolution* (1936), pp 625–6

(c) Cahier of the Third Estate of Le Revest, 1789

Cahier of grievances, complaints and representations of the said community, composed of 29 souls.

Placed on an arid soil, shackled and confined by the bonds of feudalism, confused in the maze of laws, exhausted by the multiplicity of tribunals of appeal, our most constant labours and bitter privations hardly furnish us with the means of meeting the charges of the State and the Province.

The tithe adds to these burdens and its charges form a load under which we remain crushed, moving towards the tomb through labours and sufferings; our last looks at our children are looks of grief because of their fate. The best of Kings can hear us; he will lighten our lot to attain this end.

The deputies who will elect the Third Order to attend and vote at the Estates-General of France will be expressly instructed by our deputies at the Assembly, which will be held on 27th instant at the town of Draguignan, to petition there for: the reform of the civil and criminal code; the obligation of magistrates to adjudge according to the letter of the law, without variation; the suppression of all intermediary tribunals, so that in any case whatsoever there cannot be more than two intervening judgements, of which the second should be final and without appeal; the abrogation of all judicial exemptions and privileges, of all processes derogatory to the liberty of the citizen, of bribery and corruption, of all arrests of persons otherwise than in pursuance of a warrant issued upon information or a general outcry.

His Majesty will be humbly and earnestly petitioned to maintain for his faithful provincial subjects their right to be judged only by officials of their Province, so that, on any pretext or grounds whatsoever, no provincial can be deprived of his natural justice and that no cause can be taken out of the province either to be examined or to be judged.

They will request the right for the Third Estate of whatsoever order they may be, to qualify for all military posts, honours and pensions confined to the nobility; that no exemptions can be accorded from the payment of any dues and impositions whatsoever due to the King. . . .

They will request also: a reduction in the price of salt, to make it uniform throughout the kingdom, the rate at which it now stands in this province being enormous; the power to grow tobacco on our lands; the abolition of annates; . . . the summoning and reforming of the estates of the province; the power of the Third Estate to have advocates; the right of the Third Estate to have as many members of the Estates as the first two orders combined; . . . a general tax on all property, both real and personal, to be collected in the same manner and in the same form; the diversion of the tithe to its true purpose, so that it may indeed be used for the honest and decent maintenance of the ministers of the altar, and the remainder to be divided into two portions of which one should be relinquished for the relief of the faithful subjects of His Majesty, and the other collected to be employed for enlarging military hospitals and to reward those of the Third Estate who shall deserve well of the State; the sending of money due to the King directly from the Province to the treasury of the State.

Done and concluded at Revest, 23rd. March 1789, by the inhabitants of the said community.

E. Reich, *Select Documents* (1905), pp 396–8

Questions

a   Compare the opinion of Lord Chesterfield (p 68 above) to that of the writers of extracts *a* and *b* about the circumstances favourable to revolution in France.
b   What were the 'Estates-General' (line 38) and the 'Assembly' (line 39)?
c   How does extract *c* illustrate the hatred of feudalism in France, which is mentioned in extracts *a* and *b*?
★ d   'The urge for equality'. Was this the most important cause of the French Revolution?

2   Explanations of the Revolution

(a) The transformation of the nation

The Revolution substituted a system more conformable with justice and better-suited to our times. It substituted law in the place of arbitrary will, equality in that of privilege; it delivered men from the distinction of classes, the land from the barrier of provinces, trade from the shackles of corporations and fellowships, agriculture from feudal subjection and the aggression of tithes, property from the impediment of entails, and brought everything to the condition of one state, one system of law, one people.

F. A. M. Mignet, *History of the French Revolution from 1789 to 1814* (Everyman edition, 1915), p 1

(b) Order and liberty

The new Constitution offered securities for order and liberty such as France had never enjoyed. The Revolution had begun with a Liberalism which was a passion more than a philosophy, and the first Assembly endeavoured to realise it by diminishing authority, weakening the executive and decentralising power. In the hour of peril under the Girondins the policy failed, and the Jacobins governed on the principle that power, coming from the people, ought to be concentrated in the fewest possible hands and made absolutely irresistible. Equality became the substitute of liberty, and the danger arose that the most welcome form of equality would be the equal distribution of property. . . . These schemes were at an end, and the Constitution of the Year III closes the revolutionary period.

Lord Acton, *Lectures on the French Revolution* (1910), pp 342–3

(c) Democracy and republicanism

I wish to write the political history of the Revolution from the point of view of the origin and development of Democracy and Republicanism. Democracy is the logical consequence of the principle of equality. Republicanism is the logical consequence of the principle of national sovereignty. These two consequences did not ensue at once. In place of Democracy the men of 1789 founded a middle-class government, a suffrage of property-owners. In place of the Republic, they organised a limited monarchy. Not until September 22nd did they abolish the Monarchy and create the Republic. The republican form of government lasted . . . until 1804 . . . when the government of the Republic was confined to an Emperor.

F. V. Aulard, *A Political History of the French Revolution*, trans. B. Miall (4 vols, 1910), I, Preface

(d) Salvation and freedom

The most important lesson to be drawn from this enquiry [into the nature of the French Revolution] is the incompatibility of the idea of an all-embracing and all-solving creed with liberty. The two ideals correspond to the two instincts most deeply imbedded in human nature, the yearning for salvation and the love of freedom. To attempt to satisfy both at the same time is bound to result, if not in unmitigated tyranny and serfdom, at least in the monumental hypocrisy and self-deception which are the concomitants of totalitarian democracy.

J. L. Talmon, *The Origins of Totalitarian Democracy* (1952), p 253

(e) An inevitable myth?

[We must beware of] falling into the error as though there were a single French Revolution, to be summed up in a single formula. This conception, whatever theory it is enshrined in, is the real fallacy behind all the myths of the French Revolution – the idea that there was *a* French Revolution, which you can be for or against. If in some respect the revolutionaries gave expression to the ideas of the Enlightenment, in others they underlined their application; for they stood between the rational and the romantic ages, between the Enlightenment and the religious revival, between a great wave of humanitarian sentiment and the Terror, between the idealism of 1789 and the cynicism of the Directory, between the proclamation of universal brotherhood and the wars of Napoleon. They reached the heights of heroism and descended to the depths of civil strife. A whole generation packed with significance for good and evil is summed up in the phrase 'the French Revolution'. We may pick out what we admire or dislike in it and call that the Revolution, but either is a partial verdict. Its significance in the world to-day is such that we must take all its aspects, for good or for bad, into consideration in our contemporary word-picture. . . . Every interpretation of the Revolution must in the nature of things be partial, and every partial view is a myth.

Alfred Cobban, *Aspects of the French Revolution* (1968), p 108

Questions

a Do extracts *a*, *b*, *c* and *d* suggest that these historians limited themselves to discussing the French Revolution in political and ideological terms?
b What were 'tithes' and 'entails' (lines 6–7)?
c Did Cobban imply in extract *e* that there were really several French Revolutions during these years?

* *d* Do you agree with the view that the French Revolution did not create, but only affirmed?

3 Absolutism and Terror
(a) Robespierre and Rousseau

In the earlier stages of the Revolution . . . Robespierre identified the sovereignty of the ideal Great Will, which Rousseau had proclaimed, with the actual rule of the popular will. . . . But . . . by the time of the Conventions he had discovered that the voice of
5 the people did not on all occasions accord with what he regarded as the teaching of virtue. Did it follow that the General Will was corrupted? He could not, any more than Rousseau could, accept this as a possibility. . . . But under pressure of facts . . . he ceased to think of the General Will as the actual will of the people. He
10 could still fall back upon the conception of it as an ideal will, for almost alone among the revolutionaries he understood that by the General Will meant a will which was for the general good, and which was not necessarily the will of the majority.
   In theory, and even more plainly in practice, therefore, the
15 General Will, instead of being a synonym, became a substitute for the sovereignty of the people. When the General Will became something that had to be imposed on the people through the machinery of Clubs and Committees and Tribunals, with the aid of all the forces that could be used to influence public opinion, the
20 rule of republican virtue, as Robespierre envisaged it, had become incompatible with the sovereignty of the people, and in effect a justification of minority government. . . .
   Alfred Cobban, op cit, pp 186–7

(b) Patriots and traitors

There are two sorts of people in France. One is the mass of citizens, pure, simple, inspired by justice and the love of liberty. It is these
25 virtuous people who shed their blood to establish liberty, who oppose the enemies within and overthrow the thrones of tyrants. The other is the factious and intriguing rabble – the babbling, false, crafty people, who appear everywhere, who abuse everything, who gain control of the tribunes and often of public offices, who
30 insist upon making known what advantages the *ancien régime* gave them, to mislead public opinion. These people are rogues, fools and counter-revolutionary hypocrites, who place themselves between the French people and their representatives, to deceive the one and slander the others, to impede their work and turn the most
35 beneficial laws and the most important truths against the public

well-being. As long as this impure race exists, the position of the republic will be unhappy and precarious.

    Speech of Robespierre to the Convention, 26 May 1794, *Réimpression de l'ancien Moniteur* (Paris, 1840–5), XX, p 589

(c) Responsibility for the Terror

Those who have been most forward to bring against them [the French republicans] the charge of cruelty are themselves the accomplices of their crimes. I am not apt to think that war in general has a tendency to make men more savage than they were before; yet I must confess, that I regarded the manifesto of the Duke of Brunswick, upon its first appearance, as the signal for carnage and general war. I am no advocate for French cruelties; but, to the spirit breathed, and the declarations contained, in that manifesto, I can trace much of that scene of horror and bloodshed, which has followed. . . . Posterity, feeling a just abhorrence for those cruelties which have disgraced the present age, will be better able to investigate their causes, and to discriminate their authors. They will look farther, perhaps, than to the sanguinary temper of a people who were seeking to establish their freedom; for the love of liberty is not necessarily connected with a thirst for blood. They will endeavour to discover by what means that sanguinary temper was produced: they will inquire if there was no system of proscription established against that people; if there was no combination formed, in order to deprive them of their freedom? Those who were concerned in framing the infamous manifestoes of the Duke of Brunswick, those who negotiated the Treaty of Pilnitz, the impartial voice of posterity will pronounce to have been the principal authors of all those enormities which have afflicted humanity, and desolated Europe.

    Address on the King's Speech, 21 June 1793, *Speeches of the Right Honourable Charles James Fox in the House of Commons* (6 vols, 1815), V, pp 156–7

(d) A ruthless nation

In time of innovation, all that is not new is pernicious. The military art of the monarchy no longer suits us, for we are different men and have different enemies. The power and conquests of peoples, the splendour of their politics and warfare, have always depended upon a single principle, a single powerful institution. . . . Our nation has already a national character of its own. Its military system must be different from its enemies'. Very well then: if the

French nation is terrible because of our ardour and skill, and if our enemies are clumsy, cold and slow, then our military system must be impetuous.

> Louis Saint-Just, *Rapport presenté à la Convention Nationale au nom du Comité de Salut Public, 19 du premier mois de l'an II* [10 October 1793], in E. J. Hobsbawm, *The Age of Revolution 1789–1848* (1962), p 101

(e) The enemies within

Letter of the Committee of Public Safety to their colleague, Saint-Just, on mission with the Army of the North 6 prairial year II [25 May 1794] – Liberty is exposed to new dangers. The factions revive and are more alarming than ever. The crowds demanding butter are larger and more turbulent than ever though they have the least grounds for complaint; the outbreak of a prison revolt was expected yesterday, and there are the same intrigues as were present in Hebert's time. All this is coupled with repeated attempts on the lives of the members of the Committee of Public Safety. The remnants of the factions – or rather the ever-living factions – redouble their audacity and perfidy. We fear an aristocratic rising which would be fatal to liberty. The greatest danger is in Paris. The Committee needs to unite the ideas and energy of all its members. See whether the Army of the North which, thanks in no small part to you, is on the road to victory, can spare you for a few days. Until you can return we will replace you with a patriotic representative.

> Robespierre, Prieur, Carnot, Billaud-Varenne, Barere. *Correspondance de Maximilien et Augustin Robespierre*, ed. G. Michon, 1926, no. CDX, in John Hardman (ed), *The French Revolution* (1981), p 211

(f) Economic collapse in the Year III

Paris Police Report of 30 November 1794 – Complaints and murmurs are always to be heard. The slowness of the distribution of rationed bread, the lack of flour. The high price in markets and squares of bread, firewood, wine, charcoal, vegetables and potatoes, the price of which increases every day in an alarming manner, reduces the people to a condition of wretchedness and despondency which may easily be understood.

The people's thoughts are directed towards the government by their feelings of dismay and deep misery, and nothing can be heard except expressions of ill-will against it. They are far from wishing

for the return of the Monarchy, but they willingly lend their ears
to hopes of the possibility of securing for them the end of this time
of misery and undoubted calamity.

>Archives Nationaux, F7 3688 (4), in George Rudé, *Paris and
>London in the Eighteenth Century* (1970), pp 152, 189

Questions

a   What events between 1789 and early in 1793 might have led Robespierre to change his mind about 'the voice of the people' (line 4)? What did he do to establish 'the rule of republican virtue' (line 20) during the year from July 1793 to July 1794? What was the minority whom he regarded as 'the virtuous people' (line 25)?

b   What were the Brunswick Manifesto and the Treaty of Pilnitz (lines 57–8)? Do extracts *d* and *e* support Fox's contention that these were responsible for the Terror in France?

c   Do extracts *b* and *c* suggest that the Thermidorians inherited their economic difficulties from the previous government?

★ d   Why did the Thermidorean reaction, which wished to restore the rule of law, produce a weak government unable to withstand counter-revolution?

X Napoleon in France and Abroad

Introduction

Returning from his abortive Egyptian campaign, Napoleon achieved his *coup d'état* of 18 Brumaire (9 November 1799), which overthrew the Directory, set up after the collapse of the Terror, and made him, as First Consul and then, from 1804, as Emperor, supreme ruler of France and the dependent territories secured by his conquests. This section contains Napoleon's own account of the episodes in his public proclamation and that by Louis de Bourrienne, who was Napoleon's secretary from 1797 until his dismissal in 1802, after which he became a supporter of the Bourbons (pp 106–9). These are supplemented by extracts from historians discussing the nature and significance of the *coup d'état*, of which Napoleon later said to the Comtesse de Rémusat, 'It is the epoch of my life in which I have shown most ability.' Does history support his claim? Was he justified also in insisting to the secretary of a Director that he acted as he did because, on his return to France, he found 'laws of spoliation and misery?' And was the collapse of the Constitution of the Year III really inevitable because of its own flaws?

Napoleon's reputation, when he came back from France to Egypt, was everywhere ecstatic; when his new government submitted itself to a plebiscite, it was approved by an overwhelmingly large majority; and thereafter he enjoyed great and extensive popularity in France both among the people and the soldiers. Explanations of this are given by the Comtesse de Rémusat (1780–1821), who belonged to the old aristocracy and became *dame du palais* to the Empress Josephine (whom she later called 'Madame Bonaparte'); the Vicomte de Chateaubriand (1768–1848), the writer and politician, who held office for a time under Napoleon; and Alfred de Vigny (1797–1863), the poet and author, who served for fourteen years in the French army. There follows a contribution by a modern historian and a contemporary extract about the Code Napoléon.

These extracts about those who were ruled by Napoleon are followed by passages in which he gave his own account about several aspects of his rule – his insistence that he really wanted peace in Europe; his attitude towards the subjects of his European empire, which combined the assertion that he wished to contribute towards their welfare with a determination to suppress any opposition to his rule; and, finally, his claims about his career and achievements, which he expressed during the last years of his life on the island of St Helena, written in his diary, and in conversation with Emmanuel, Comte de las Casas (1766–1842), who shared the first year of Napoleon's exile there and later published his memoirs of that time. This was to be the basis of the future 'Napoleonic Legend'; but judgement upon it was delivered by a Dutch historian, who made a thorough examination of two centuries of biographical writing about him (p 119 below).

Such material raises important questions about Napoleon and his rule. To what extent did he establish a military despotism? Who were the classes which most benefited from the Empire? And what political power did they actually possess under him? What part was played in sustaining or weakening his government by honours and titles, the Concordat with the Papacy, conscription and taxation? Was there any real improvement in the general economic condition of France during those years? And, finally, what was there in the outlook of the French people which made his rule possible and popular? Did he enjoy universal support or only from certain sections of the population of the country? Was it always as strong as ever or had it begun to decline before his downfall?

1   The Coup d'état of Brumaire, 1799

(a) Napoleon's public proclamation

19th Brumaire, 11 o'clock P.M.

To the People:
Frenchmen, on my return to France I found division reigning among all the authorities. They agreed only on this single point,
5   that the constitution was half destroyed and was unable to protect liberty.

Each party in turn came to me, confided to me their designs, imparted their secrets, and requested my support. But I refused to be the man of a party.
10   The Council of Ancients appealed to me. I answered their appeal. A plan of general restoration had been concerted by men whom the nation has been accustomed to regard as the defenders of liberty, equality and property. This plan required calm deliberation, free from all influence and all fear. The Ancients therefore resolved
15   upon the removal of the legislative bodies to St Cloud. They placed at my disposal the force necessary to secure their independence. I was bound, in duty to my fellow-citizens, to the soldiers perishing in our armies, and to the national glory acquired at the cost of so much blood, to accept the command.
20   The Council assembled at St Cloud. Republican troops guaran-

teed their safety from without, but assassins created terror within. Many deputies in the Council of Five Hundred, armed with stilettos and pistols, spread the menace of death around them.

The plans which ought to have been developed were withheld. The majority of the Council was disorganised, the boldest orators were disconcerted, and the futility of submitting any salutary proposition was quite evident.

I proceeded, filled with indignation and chagrin, to the Council of Ancients. I besought them to carry their noble designs into execution. I directed their attention to the evils of the nation, which were their motives for conceiving those designs. They concurred in giving me new proofs of their unanimous goodwill.

I presented myself before the Council of the Five Hundred alone, unarmed, my head uncovered, just as the Ancients had received and applauded me. My object was to restore to the majority the expression of its will and to secure to it its power.

The stilettos which had menaced the deputies were instantly raised against their deliverer. Twenty assassins rushed upon me and aimed at my breast. The grenadiers of the Legislative Body, whom I had left at the door of the hall, ran forward and placed themselves between me and the assassins. One of these brave grenadiers had his clothes pierced by a stiletto. They bore me out.

At the same moment cries of 'Outlaw him!' were raised against the defender of the law. It was the horrid cry of assassins against the power destined to repress them. They crowded around the president [Lucien Bonaparte] uttering threats. With arms in their hands, they commanded him to declare me outlawed. I was informed of this. I ordered him to be rescued from their fury, and six grenadiers of the legislative body brought him out. Immediately afterwards some grenadiers of the legislative body charged the hall and cleared it.

The seditious, thus intimidated, dispersed and fled. The majority, freed from their assailants, returned freely and peaceably into the hall, listened to the propositions for the public safety, deliberated, and drew up the salutary resolution which will become the new and provisional law of the republic.

Frenchmen, you will doubtless recognise in this conduct the zeal of a soldier of liberty, of a citizen devoted to the republic. Conservative, liberal and judicial ideas resumed their sway upon the dispersion of those seditious persons who had domineered in the councils, and who proved themselves the most odious and contemptible of men.

Bonaparte.

Corresp. Nap. Ier, VI, p 5f, in J. H. Robinson, *Readings in European History*, II, pp 478–80

(b) Another account

The sitting of the Ancients, under the presidency of Lemercier, commenced at one o'clock.

A warm discussion took place upon the situation of affairs, the resignations of the members of the Directory and the immediate election of others. Great heat and agitation prevailed during the debate. Intelligence of what was going forward was every minute carried to Bonaparte, and he determined to enter the hall and take part in the discussion.

He entered in a hasty and angry way, which did not give me a favourable foreboding of what he was about to say. We passed through a narrow passage to the centre of the hall; our backs were turned to the doors. Bonaparte had the President on his right. He could not see him full in the face. I was close to the generals on his right. Bertheir was at his left.

All the speeches, which have been subsequently passed off as having been delivered by Bonaparte on this occasion, differ from each other; as well they may, for he delivered none, unless his confused answers to the President, which were alike devoid of dignity and sense, are to be called a speech. He talked of his 'brothers in arms' and the 'frankness of a soldier'.

The questions of the President followed each other rapidly; they were clear; but it is impossible to conceive anything more confused or worse delivered than the ambiguous and perplexed replies of Bonaparte. He talked without end of 'volcanoes, secret agitations, victories, a violated constitution'. . . . Next followed the words 'liberty – equality', though it was evident he had not come to St Cloud for the sake of either.

No sooner did he utter these words than a member of the Ancients named, I think, Linglet, abruptly interrupting him, exclaimed: 'You forget the constitution'.

His countenance immediately lighted up, yet nothing could be distinguished but – 'The 18th Fructidor – the 30th Prairial – hypocrites – intriguers – I will disclose all – I will resign my power when the danger which threatens the Republic shall have passed away'. Bonaparte, believing all his assertions to be admitted, assumed a little confidence and accused the two Directors, Barras and Moulin, of having proposed to put him at the head of a party whose object was to oppose all men professing liberal ideas.

At these words, the falsehood of which was obvious, a great turmoil arose in the hall. A general committee was loudly called for to hear the disclosures. . . .

Bonaparte was then required to enter into the particulars of his accusation against Barras and Moulin and of the proposals which had been made to him: 'You must no longer conceal anything'.

Embarrassed by these interruptions and interrogatories, Bonaparte believed that he was completely lost. Instead of giving an explanation of what he had said, he began to make fresh accusations; and against whom? The Council of Five Hundred, who, he said, wished for 'scaffolds, revolutionary committees and a complete overthrow of everything'. Violent murmurings arose, and his language became more and more incoherent and inconsequential. He addressed himself at one moment to the representatives of the people, who were quite overcome by astonishment; at another to the military in the courtyard, who could hear him; then, by an unaccountable transition, he spoke of 'the thunderbolts of war', and added that he was 'attended by the god of war and the god of fortune'. The President with great calmness told him that he saw nothing, absolutely nothing, upon which the Council could deliberate; and that there was vagueness in all he had said. 'Explain yourself; reveal the plot in which you say you were urged to join.'

Bonaparte repeated again the same things. But only those who were present can form any idea of his manner. There was not the slightest connection in what he stammered out. Bonaparte was no orator. It may well be supposed that he was more accustomed to the din of war than to the discussions of the tribunes. He was more at home before a battery than before a president's chair.

Perceiving the bad effect which this unconnected babbling produced on the assembly, as well as the embarrassment of Bonaparte, I said in a low voice, pulling gently the skirt of his coat, 'Withdraw, General, you know not what you are saying'.

I made signs to Berthier, who was on his left, to second me in persuading him to leave the hall; then suddenly, and all at once, after having stammered out a few more words, he turned round exclaiming, 'Let those who love me, follow me!'

The sentinels at the door offered no opposition to his passing. . . . It is hard to say what would have happened if, on seeing the General retire, the President had said: 'Grenadiers, let no one pass!' Probably, instead of sleeping next day at the Luxembourg, he might have ended his career on the Place de la Révolution.

Louis de Bourrienne, *Memoirs of Napoléon Bonaparte* (4 vols, 1836), I, pp 246–8

(c) Brumaire and Liberty (1)

Among the legends which have found acceptance about the 18th Brumaire, none is more completely erroneous than that of the Assassination of Liberty. It was long an historical commonplace to represent Bonaparte as shattering with one blow of his sword a truly lawful state of affairs and in the *Orangerie* of St Cloud stifling with the roll of his drums the last years of French liberty. It is no longer permissible to respect that solemn absurdity, Bonaparte can be blamed for not having founded Liberty, he cannot be accused of having overthrown it for the excellent reason that he nowhere found it in being on his return to France. . . . Directorial anarchy, parliamentary noise, these things were becoming abhorrent to the generals. This regime of impotent babblers revolted their manliness; their gorge rose at last with disgust against the malodorous untidiness of the revolutionaries.

Count Albert Vaudal, *L'Avènement de Bonaparte* (1903), in Peter Geyl, *Napoleon: For and Against* (1958), pp 214–15

(d) Brumaire and liberty (2)

It is sometimes argued that the coup was necessary, that the government of the Directory was too impossible to be allowed to live. Napoleon, of course, argued this himself. On St Helena he said: 'People are still engaged in abstract deliberations as to whether our action of 18th Brumaire was a legal or a criminal one. At the best, however, these are but theories suitable for books or public orators, and which disappear before the face of sheer necessity. It is like condemning a sailor for chopping off a mast to escape shipwreck. The perpetrators of this great *coup d'état* could reply to their accusers as did the Roman of old: "Our act is justified in that we saved the Republic; let us therefore render thanks to the gods".'

There is strength in this argument, although it is by no means a quibble to point out that whatever 18th Brumaire did or did not achieve, it certainly did *not* save the Republic. The answer, however, surely is that so long as some form of representative government existed, there had always been the possibility of reform and of the retention of individual liberty.

After 18th Brumaire this was no longer possible. The genie was out of the bottle; and it took all Europe fifteen years and more to put him back again.

D. J. Goodspeed, *Bayonets at St Cloud* (1965), pp 171–2

(e) The consulate

The authors of this *coup d'état* did not think of destroying the Republic; they only wished to strengthen the government by reducing from five to three the number of its members and preserving the republican membership of the chief offices of the State by distributing it among assemblies composed by means of reducing elections to a formality. They nominated provisionally *three consuls* (a name taken following the fashion of the times from Roman antiquity) and formed two commissions charged with

185 drawing up a constitution. But Bonaparte, one of the consuls, changed the plan so as to secure supreme power for himself. He was called *first consul* and alone invested with 'executive power' which gave him the control of the whole government and the right to appoint officials. The 'legislative power' was shared among four
190 assemblies each charged with a single function: the *Council of State* to prepare laws, the *Tribunate* to discuss them, the *Legislative Body* to vote on them and the *Senate* to maintain the Constitution. All the members received quite exalted treatment for the time. A proclamation indicated the principle of this regime: 'Its powers
195 will be sovereign and permanent. The Revolution preserves the principles with which it began; it is finished.'

   Charles Seignobos, *Histoire sincère de la nation française* (1944), pp 257–8

Questions

a   How is Napoleon represented as acting differently during the 18th Brumaire in extracts *a* and *b*?
b   What were the Council of Ancients (line 10) and the Council of Five Hundred (line 22), 18th Fructidor and 30th Prairial (line 94)? Where was the Orangery of St Cloud (line 146)? Why would Napoleon's fate have been different if he had gone to the Place de la Révolution instead of to the Luxembourg (line 140)?
c   Did the 18th Brumaire destroy liberty in France or save the country from disorder?
★ d   How far did Napoleon succeed in his declared aim of making his new government one of reconciliation?

2 Napoleon's Supporters

(a) Law and order

I can understand how it was that men worn out by the turmoil of the Revolution, and afraid of that liberty which had long been associated with death, looked for repose under the domination of an able ruler on whom fortune seemingly resolved to smile.
5 I can conceive that they regarded his elevation as a decree of destiny and firmly believed that in the irrevocable they should find peace. I may confidently assert that those persons believed quite sincerely that Bonaparte, whether as consul or emperor, would exert his authority to oppose the intrigues of faction and would save us from
10 the perils of anarchy.
  None dared to utter the word 'republic', so deeply had the Terror stained that name, and the government of the Directory had perished in the contempt with which its chiefs were regarded. The return of the Bourbons could only be brought about by the aid of

revolution; and the slightest disturbance terrified the French people, in whom enthusiasm of every kind seemed dead. Besides, the men in whom they had trusted had one after another deceived them; and as, this time, they were yielding to force, they were at least certain they were not deceiving themselves.

The belief, or rather the error, that only despotism could at that epoch maintain order in France was very widespread. It became the mainstay of Bonaparte; and it is due to him to say that he also believed it. The factions played into his hands by imprudent attempts which he turned to his own advantage. He had some grounds for his belief that he was necessary; France believed it, too; and he even succeeded in persuading foreign sovereigns that he constituted a barrier against republican influences, which, but for him, might spread widely. At the moment when Bonaparte placed the imperial crown upon his head there was not a king in Europe who did not believe that he wore his own crown more securely because of that event. Had the new emperor granted a liberal constitution, the peace of nations and of kings might really have been forever secured.

Claire, Comtesse de Rémusat, *Memoirs* (Eng. trans., 1880), pp 160f.

(b) Winning the hearts of his soldiers

Bonaparte's reception by the troops was nothing short of rapturous. It was well worth seeing how he talked to the soldiers, – how he questioned them one after the other respecting their campaigns or their wounds, taking particular interest in the men who had accompanied him to Egypt. I have heard Madame Bonaparte say that her husband was in the constant habit of poring over the list of what are called the *cadres* of the army at night before he slept. He would go to sleep repeating the names of the corps and even of some of the individuals who composed them; he kept these names in a corner of his memory, and this habit came to his aid when he wanted to recognise a soldier and to give him the pleasure of a cheering word from his general. He spoke to the subalterns in a tone of good-fellowship, which delighted them all, as he reminded them of their common feats of arms.

Ibid., p 36

(c) The love of equality

One may wonder by what magic spell Bonaparte, so aristocratic and so hostile to the mob, came to win the popularity which he enjoyed: for that forger of yokes has certainly remained popular with a nation whose pretension it was to raise altars to liberty and equality; this is the solution to the enigma:

Daily experience shows that the French are instinctively attracted by power; they have no love for liberty; equality is their idol. Now equality and tyranny have secret connexions. In these two respects, Napoleon had his fountain-head in the hearts of the French, militarily inclined towards power, democratically enamoured of a dead level. Mounting the throne, he seated the common people beside him; a proletarian king, he levelled the ranks of society, not by lowering but by raising them: levelling-down would have pleased plebeian envy more: levelling-up was more flattering to its pride. French vanity was puffed up too by the superiority which Bonaparte gave us over the rest of Europe.

The Memoirs of Chateaubriand, ed. and trans. Robert Baldrick (1965), p 329

(d) The call of glory

I belong to the generation born with the century, who, nourished by the bulletins of the Emperor, always had a drawn sword before their eyes and was about to take it up at the very moment when France sheathed it in the Bourbon's scabbard. . . .

Towards the end of the Empire, I was a heedless schoolboy. The war was present in the school, the drum deafened my ears to the masters' voices, and the mysterious voice of the books spoke to us only in a cold and pedantic language. Logarithms and figures of speech were in our eyes only steps to mount to the star of the Legion of Honour, the most beautiful star in the sky for children.

No thoughts could occupy our heads which were ceaselessly filled with the noise of the cannon and the bells of the *Te Deum*! When one of our companions, who had left the college a few months earlier, reappeared in a hussar's uniform with his arm in a sling, we blushed at our books and threw them at our masters. The masters themselves never stopped reading us the bulletins of the Grand Army, and our cries of '*Vive L'Empereur*' interrupted Tacitus and Plato. Our teachers resembled heralds-at-arms, our classrooms were barracks, our games were manoeuvres, and our examinations were inspections. . . .

War seemed to us so magnificently the state of our country that, when we escaped from school, we threw ourselves into the army, borne along by the torrent of our aspirations; we could not believe in the lasting calm of peace. It did not seem that we were risking anything in pretending to rest or that immobility was a serious evil in France. This impression remained with us as long as the Restoration. Each year brought the hope of a war; and we dare not

give up the sword for fear that the day of our resignation would be the eve of a campaign. So we spun out and lost our precious years, dreaming of the field of battle on the *Champ de Mars*, and exhausting our strength and useless enemy on parades and private
95 quarrels.
   Alfred de Vigny, *Servitude et Grandeur Militaires* (Librairie Grund, Paris, n.d.,), pp 7, 12–14

(e) A new elite

Historians seem to be agreeing that in the 1770s and 1780s a new elite of notables was emerging in France as the product of the fusion of noble landowners; noble landowners who were entering business; bankers, merchants and a very few industrialists, who
100 generally owned land; and professional men. From 1788 fusion was brutally interrupted by the fights over noble privilege and by the events of emigration, war and terror, but once legal privileges had been abolished and the superheated exaltation of the great revolutionary days had cooled, the process of fusion was resumed
105 during the last days of the Directory and continued under Napoleon. Napoleon himself, for his own purposes, fostered the process by reopening the gates of France to *émigrés*, by adding in his top generals and administrators and endowing them with lands, and by instituting the Legion of Honour, a consular and imperial court
110 and an imperial liberty.
   Harold T. Parker, 'Napoleon Reconsidered', *French Historical Studies*, XV, no. 1 (Spring 1987), p 150

(f) The Code Napoléon

State Counsellor Portalis, 1804 – To-day uniform laws will remove all absurdities and dangers; civil order will cement political order. We will no longer by Provençals, Bretons or Alsacians, but only Frenchmen. Names have a greater influence than one believes on
115 men's thoughts and actions. Uniformity is not only established in the relations that should exist between the parts of the State; it is also established in the relations that ought to exist between individuals. Formerly humiliating distinctions, which political privilege had introduced among persons, had also invaded civil rights.
120 There was a law of succession for nobles, and another for those who were not; there were privileged properties which the latter could not own without a dispensation from the monarch. All these traces of barbarism have been removed; the law is the common mother of all citizens; she gives equal protection to all. One of the

125 great achievements of the new code is also to have brought to an end all civil differences between men who profess different beliefs. Religious opinions are free. The law no longer seeks to force consciences; it seeks to follow the great principle that it should tolerate whom God tolerates. So it wishes only to know citizens,
130 just as nature only knows men.
There has been no attempt to introduce dangerous novelties into the new legislation. All has been preserved from the old laws which can be reconciled with the present order of society; the stability of marriage has been upheld; wise rules for the government of families
135 have been provided; the authority of fathers has been re-established; every way of assuring the submission of children has been brought back; a proper latitude has been allowed to the charity of testators; all the general principles of agreements have been expounded and also those which establish the particular nature of each contract;
140 care has been given to the maintenance of good customs, the reasonable freedom of trade and every object which concerns civil society.

M. D. Dalloz, *Répertoire alphabétique méthodique de législation* (36 vols, 1853), XXX, pp 222f.

Questions

a Consider how Napoleon was able to maintain the power and prestige of his army, consulting also the extracts on pages 60–1.

b What were the Grand Army (line 80), the Legion of Honour (line 73) and the *Champ de Mars* (line 93)?

c 'A husband owes protection to his wife; a wife obedience to her husband' – 'A father who, for very serious reasons, is displeased with the conduct of a child . . . can have him imprisoned for one month [if under sixteen] . . . for six months [if sixteen or over]' – (The Code Napoléon). Did the Code seek the support of the citizens who were dominant politically and socially?

* d Was Napoleon justified in claiming that he did not destroy the Revolution, but rather fulfilled it?

3 In his Own Words

(a) A denial of aggression

All my victories and all my conquests were won in self-defence. This is a truth which time will render every day more evident. Europe never ceased from warring against France, against French principles and against me, so we had to strike down in order not
5 to be struck down. The coalition continued without interruption,

be it open or in secret, admitted or denied; it was there in
permanence. It depended solely on the allies to give us peace.

. . .

At Amiens [in 1802] I imagined in all good faith that I had settled
France's destiny and my own. . . . I was planning to devote myself
10 exclusively to the administration, and I believe that I could have
worked wonders. I might have achieved the moral conquest of
Europe, just as I have been on the verge of accomplishing it by
arms.

P. Geyl, op cit, pp 252, 274

(b) The benefits of his empire (1)

Napoleon to the Council of State, August 1799 – My policy is to
15 govern men as the great majority wish to be governed. That I
believe is the way to recognise the sovereignty of the people. It
was as a Catholic that I won the war in the Vendée, as a Moslem
that I established myself in Egypt, and as an Ultramontane that I
won the confidence of the Italians. If I were governing Jews, I
20 should rebuild the temple of Solomon.

J. M. Thompson, *Napoleon Bonaparte: His Rise and Fall*
(1958), p 172

(c) The benefits of his empire (2)

Napoleon to Jerome, King of Westphalia, 1805 – Your throne will
never be firmly established except upon the trust and affection of
the common people. What German opinion impatiently demands
is that men of no rank, but of marked ability, shall have an equal
25 claim upon your favour and upon your employment, and that
every trace of serfdom, or of a feudal hierarchy, between the
sovereign and the lowest class of his subjects, shall be done away
with. The benefits of the Code Napoléon, public trial and the
introduction of juries, will be the leading features of your
30 Government. And to tell you the truth, I count more upon their
effects, for the extension and consolidation of your rule, than upon
the most resounding victories.

R. C. Bridges, P. Dukes, J. D. Hargreaves and W. Scott
(eds), *Nations and Empires* (1969), p 88

(d) Its other aspect (1)

Napoleon to Charles-François Lebrun, Ligurian Republic.

Boulogne Camp, August 11 1805

I was sorry to see your decree prohibiting the recruitment of sailors at Genoa. . . . I have mobilised the fleet at Genoa just in order to get sailors, and yet the only three frigates I have in the harbour are not manned. Why do you suppose I annexed Genoa, and admitted her to the many advantages she gains by membership of my Empire? It was not for the money I can get out of her, nor for the reinforcements she provides for my armies on land: my only object was to secure 15 000 more sailors. It is therefore contravening the whole spirit of the annexation to pass a decree disavowing naval recruitment. . . . These people will never be really Gallicized until I have my sailors on board my ships. . . . I cannot agree with you that professional sailors are no use – that they are only good for coastal trade and terrified of going to sea in a ship of war. If so we must find some way of terrifying them still more. I am afraid you have been influenced, in your management of this business, by the fear of offending the Genoese. Never mind about that. Whether they wish it or not, I must have them on my vessels; or else I shall be forced to extreme measures, such as putting an embargo on their coastal trade. . . . Nations cannot be governed by weakness; it only does them harm. . . . As for those who say that this measure will make the Genoese troublesome and discontented – I am not the man for such talk. I know well enough what the Genoese are capable of. Do people think I am already so decrepit that they can frighten me with the Genoese? There is only one answer to this despatch – sailors and again sailors. . . .

Corresp. Nap. Ier., XI, no. 9064, in J. M. Thompson, *Letters of Napoleon*, pp 123–5

(e) Its other aspect (2)

Napoleon to Marshal Alexandre Berthier, Prince of Neuchâtel.

Saint-Cloud, August 5, 1806

I imagine that you have arrested the Augsburg and Nuremburg booksellers. My intention is to bring them before a court-martial and to have them shot within 24 hours [for circulating a tract deploring the French occupation of Germany]. It is no ordinary crime to spread defamatory writings in places occupied by the French armies and to incite the inhabitants against them. It is high treason. The sentence must declare that, since wherever an army may be, it is the duty of its commander to see to its safety, such and such individuals, having been found guilty of trying to rouse the inhabitants of Suabia against the French army, are condemned to death.

You will parade the guilty in the centre of a division and appoint seven colonels to be their judges. In the sentence, you must mention that the defamatory writings originally came from the booksellers Kupper of Vienna and Enrich of Linz, and that they are condemned to death in their absence; the sentence to be carried out, if they are captured, wherever the French troops may happen to be. You are to have the sentence published all over Germany.
Corresp. Nap. Ier., XIII, no. 10597, in ibid., p 122

(f) His verdict on himself (1)

Saint Helena, 1 May 1816 – They may change and chop and suppress, but after all they will find it pretty difficult to make me disappear altogether. A French historian cannot very easily avoid dealing with the Empire; and, if he has a heart, he will give me back something of my own. I sealed the gulf of anarchy, and I unravelled chaos. I purified the revolution, raised the people, and strengthened monarchy. I stimulated every ambition, rewarded every merit, and pushed back the bounds of glory! All that amounts to something!

3 March 1817 – In spite of all the libels, I have no fear whatever about my fame. Posterity will do me justice. The truth will be known; and the good I have done will be compared with the faults I have committed. I am not uneasy as to the result. Had I succeeded, I would have died with the reputation of the greatest man that ever existed. As it is, although I have failed, I shall be considered as an extraordinary man: my elevation was unparalleled, because unaccompanied by crime. I have fought fifty pitched battles, almost all of which I have won. I have framed and carried into effect a code of laws that will bear my name to the most distant posterity. I raised my self from nothing to be the most powerful monarch in the world. Europe was at my feet. I have always been of the opinion that the sovereignty lay in the people. In fact, the imperial government was a kind of republic. Called to the head of it by the voice of the nation, my maxim was, *la carrière est ouverte aux talents* without distinction of birth or fortune, and this system of equality is the reason that your oligarchy hates me so much.
R. M. Johnston, *The Corsican: A Diary of Napoleon's Life in His Own Words* (1910), pp 457, 492

(g) His verdict on himself (2)

St Helena, 24 August 1816 – The cause of the age was victorious, the revolution accomplished; the only point in question was to reconcile it with what it had not destroyed. But that task belonged to me; I had for a long time being making preparations for it, *at the expense, perhaps, of my popularity.* No matter. I became the arch of the old and new alliance, the natural mediator between the ancient and modern order of things. I maintained the principles and possessed the confidence of the one; I had identified myself with the other. I belonged to them both; I should have acted conscientiously in favour of each.

Comte de Las Cases, *The Journal of the Private Life and Conversations of the Emperor Napoleon at Saint Helena* (8 vols, 1823), V, pp 265–7

(h) A historian's verdict

He was a dictator who attempted to break with new legislation what resistance was left in the old society; who intensified his power in the State by means of a centralised adminstration; who suppressed, not only all organised influence or control and expression of opinion, but free thought itself; who hated the intellect, and who entered upon a struggle with the Church which he had first attempted to enslave, and who thought that with censorship, police and propaganda, he would be able to fashion the mind to his wish.

He was a conqueror with whom it was impossible to live; who could not help turning an ally into a vassal or at least interpreting the relationship to his own exclusive advantage; who decorated his lust of conquest with fine-sounding phrases of progress and civilisation; and who at last, in the name of the whole of Europe, which was to look to him for order and peace, presumed to brand England as the universal disturber and enemy.

P. Geyl, op cit, p 279

Questions

a   'They are like children, who require rewards for docility, but the rod for defiance' (Napoleon). Was this his policy towards his conquered subjects in Europe?
b   What did Napoleon mean by *la carrière est ouverte aux talents* (line 104), and how did he put it into effect?
c   Do you consider that extract *h* is more credible than Napoleon's statements about himself?
d   'He was as great a man as can be without morality' (De Tocqueville). Discuss this judgement upon Napoleon.